SO-ARN-647

Holding Another's Hand

Holding Another's Hand

FACING THE TRANSITION CALLED DEATH

Edited by
Richard Robinson

JUNIPER
SPRINGS
P R E S S

PUBLISHED BY

Juniper Springs Press

P.O. Box 1385, Apple Valley, CA 92307

Internet: www.JuniperSpringsPress.com

For information, e-mail: Publish@JuniperSpringsPress.com

© 2005 by Richard Robinson

ISBN 0-9678876-1-5

Library of Congress Control Number: 2004105822

All rights reserved. No part of this book, except "Flow" (page 119), may be reproduced in any form or by any electronic or mechanical means, including information storage and retrieval systems, without permission in writing from the publisher, except by a reviewer, who may quote brief passages in a review. "Flow," as presented on page 119, may be reproduced and distributed freely, provided the permission statement at the bottom of page 119 appears on all duplicated copies.

"A Valentine to Remember" (page 56) © 1998 W. Brugh Joy, M.D. All rights reserved. Used with permission.

Printed and bound in the United States of America

First printing: January 2005

I dedicate this book to

ELISABETH KUBLER-ROSS

for all of her wisdom and work
with the dying, with hospice,
with palliative caregivers,
and
. . . for her compassionate heart, her guiding light . . .

"We will hold your hand until it is taken from the other side."

Benedictine Nuns—Eibingen, Germany

GRATEFUL APPRECIATION

My most sincere gratitude and appreciation to four individuals who stepped forward to help and guide me with this book/project:

Dr. Margaret Stortz, my personal spiritual guide and teacher.

John Thatcher, another close friend, educated in matters of the heart, mind, and soul.

Louise Hay, a longtime friend and guiding Star in collective healing work.

John Niendorff, a gift from Spirit, come to lead, guide, and nurture me with this book project as my editor.

I am grateful to each for their help and support.

CONTENTS

Shared Teachings

Sharing Recollections

Shared Reflections on Service

INTRODUCTION

My purpose and intentions for this book are many-faceted. For many years now, I have been generating funds for various care and support organizations by producing lectures, workshops, and other gatherings of all sizes, where particular teachings or compassionate-care trainings were brought forward. Revenues were generated by contributions from the attendees for AIDS caregivers' trainings, services, and hospice care. I donated my time as well as the necessary production costs. With the helping hands of many friends, these events generated more contribution dollars, larger audiences, and more inspirational teachings than I could have as an individual with just two hands and one checkbook.

The same conceptual approach and intentions have brought about *Holding Another's Hand*. Here you will find many stories of how we can deal with death, how we can become more fully aware of our feelings about our death, and how we can be present for one another at the time of transition from this Life experience to the next Life experience. My sincere hope and my intentions are that this book will lift and carry healing words and solace to wherever and whomever they are needed and called for.

May the words, thoughts, and insights on these pages relieve all fear and doubts in me, in all caregivers, and in those who now step forward to hold another's hand. May this book help us all open to the bigger view of Life and a sense of our Spiritual Continuum . . . of Life transitioning into Life.

And I pray that we all, when called upon, will participate in this mystery as caregivers and providers of support, comfort, and solace . . . *holding another's hand.*

SHARED
TEACHINGS

*True knowledge is to see one changeless Life in
all lives and in the Separate, One Inseparable.*

The Bhagavad-Gita

SHARED TEACHINGS

BAMBI AND ME

When I was just a child, sometime in the early 1940s, I was taken to see the movie *Bambi*. My mother must not have taken me herself, because to this day she says I was "too young" to see that movie. To me this means it either disturbed me or it disturbed *her* for me to view the death of Bambi's mother.

I do remember that this movie left me with an intense fear and wonderment at the mystery of fire. I was scared by it back then when I was a tot, and it continued to scare me all through my childhood years. To this day, fire is a big unsolved "secret" mystery for me. But the death of Bambi's mother by the men with guns was not the terrifying imprint that remained in my consciousness. The fire was.

What may have been my first viewing of death revealed another fear embedded deep within my young psyche, that of *separation*. Bambi's loss of his mother was very sad, and I probably cried for Bambi, for his aloneness and the *separation* forced upon him. I believe I never anguished or cried over his mother's death, for she had gone to "heaven," as I had been taught in those years. It was little Bambi who needed help and protection in that forest-world, and *he* got my childhood tears.

After years of all kinds of therapy, transformational teachings, and metaphysical studies, I now believe I did not come into this world with a fear of death. While I have the usual inner blender full of phobias, angst, worries, and woes, I believe the Creator and Great Spirit let me in here without this one major fear—of death.

My worries, fears, and sadness for Bambi were and still are for his separation, for his being left alone in this world at

3

such a tender young age. I am sure this sent terror through my heart and soul. Bambi's mother was safe in another place, a place called "heaven," but poor little Bambi with wobbly legs was stuck down here! That brings me right to where I *do* have pain and sorrow around the transition we call death. For me death means separation, often leaving unresolved issues and unfinished business—an uncompleted mission here on Earth.

A tough path to be on for learning about life—so young, alone!

As have many of you who are reading this now, I have been to many memorials, funerals, and candlelight celebrations of lives gone on to another place, another plane. My tears flow freely, but not due to fear about where or what has become of the departed person. I cry over the loss, the separation from their friends, including myself. I cry over *all* the "unfinished business," unfulfilled dreams, and difficult roads that the lovers, friends, parents, sisters, and brothers walk along as they grieve their loss. This is the tough stuff for me surrounding life's end on this plane. My concern is over a perception of separation, not any fear regarding the next destination.

Going into the "Great Unknown," whether in a really spectacular way or just by quietly stepping across into the next plane of Life, will be a new beginning. I hope I will welcome it whenever the time comes for me . . . .

Throughout these pages, I, along with many other contributors, share stories about the death experiences of parents, husbands/wives, lovers, relatives, and friends. My hope is that our insights and gentle suggestions will assist all of the children, grandchildren, relatives, friends, and other caregivers who step forward to hold the hands of those who are leaving us.

Richard Robinson, RScP, *caregiver, student.*

CROSSING BOUNDARIES

At the heart of all spiritual practices is the skill of standing at a boundary and enabling a crossing to take place. The boundary may be between the sacred and the personal, and that which crosses is grace and a vision of God in all things and all moments. The boundary may be between ourselves and another, and that which crosses is love; the boundary may be between the actual and potential, and that which crosses is vision and inspiration, creativity and skill. Or the boundary can be between life and death, embodiment and disembodiment, and that which crosses is faith, wonderment, and the soul.

Death may seem the most challenging boundary of all, but all boundaries are challenging; all are scary, for all represent a contact with the unknown "out there" and the unknown within us. They inspire questions: *"What in me can rise to make this crossing?"* and *"What will become of me when I do?"*

To embrace boundaries, to stand at the edge in our lives—even between life and death—and to enable crossings to occur with grace and presence is to be at the center of all spiritual practice. It is to be the warrior, the knight, the priest, the shaman, the monk, the nun, the servant of the sacred. It is to become love, which is the ultimate bridge through which all things meet and become one.

David Spangler, author, mystic, teacher.

REMARKS ON THE PASSING OF A FRIEND . . .

Last year my wife Brenda and I were part of a group being led up a mountain in Glacier Park, Montana. Our guide was a park ranger, and our destination was a beautiful, remote, granite chalet that could only be reached on foot or by horseback. Legend has it that the best pies in the world are served at this inn.

After four or five hours on this climb, it became apparent that Brenda and I were too tired to continue up the mountain. We had not trained for the altitude and the length of the hike. When we stopped to rest, we bade the others to go on ahead. They continued up the trail and soon had passed beyond our physical sight, ready to continue their journey onward and upward. We were not ready then, and returned to the lodge at the base of the mountain.

We missed their company and were sorry we would not taste the heavenly confection of the pies at the inn. Although we could no longer see the climbers, we felt certain they were safe, sound, and happy. They were in the hands of a skilled ranger. They were simply out of sight for a time. Later that evening they returned to the lodge, and we were together again.

And so it is with our loved ones who have passed from this physical realm. They were ready to continue their journey up the mountain to a new place. Though we cannot see them now, we can be certain they are well, for they have a wonderful Guide to lead the way. We shall be together again, for there is no separation in Spirit.

It is natural to desire to continue the journey with our loved ones. We grieve when one we care for goes on ahead, but let us not dwell on the sense of loss. Our loved one was ready to journey forward, and we would not hold him back from his highest good.

To our friend, we say, "Godspeed on your way. We know you are well. With the passing of time, and our faith in God, and in your spiritual progress, our heaviness of heart will also pass. We shall be together again in another lodge of our Father's. We shall be there to meet you, by and by. We know all is well." And so it is.

Rev. John Strickland, Minister, former Vice President of Unity and former Director of Silent Unity. (This was presented by Rev. John at a friend's memorial service then published in Unity's Daily Word magazine.)

MY THOUGHTS ON DEATH

There was an instant in time when you were no-where. Then in one holy instant you went from no-where to now-here.

There will be another holy instant when you will go from now-here to no-where. We call that moment death. Yet you— the divine, changeless, eternal, invisible you—will live on.

Someday your physical self will probably rest beneath a tombstone that records the date of your birth and the date of your death. But your inner soul knows you are eternal. You are formless in that part of yourself and have no boundaries. Without boundaries there is no birth, no death. What was born will die, what was never born can never die. Your sacred self was never born! Your sacred self will never die!

Surrender! This involves an act of the heart. The act of surrendering takes place in a moment. Let go of your conflict with what is and what can be, and surrender. Stop asking, "Why me?"

Accept the fact that your body will die *and* that you are eternal. Surrender to this fact when someone dies and stop telling yourself that their death shouldn't have happened the way it did. You can surrender and accept *and* you can grieve.

Notice any repetitious inner dialogue about the horrors and tragedies of the world. Surrender and let Go(d). This doesn't mean you will rejoice in the suffering of others. It means you will not focus your inner divine energy on suffering. You will be freer to help eliminate suffering.

Millions of people die every day, and millions more show up here on our planet. It is a play of continuous entrances and exits. All of your opinions about how that should be taking place are nothing more than notions that you have of how God should be orchestrating this play.

But it is all perfect, even the part that you dislike or judge as bad. Surrender and know that you too are one of those characters who made an entrance and will experience an exit.

But also know that your soul is eternal, and that is who you truly are. Surrender now! It only takes an instant.

The opposite of fear is not courage—it is love. When you experience love within, you have no guilt and no fear. You know that everything you are experiencing is in order, including your woes, which are your greatest teachers, and the death of your body, which is ordained for all the world of the manifest. You have nothing to fear unless you listen to your ego encouraging fear and dismissing God.

Wayne W. Dyer, Ph.D., teacher of Transformational Wisdom, author.

When we came into this life, we were met by loving friends who cared for us until we were able to care for ourselves. Judging the future by the past, and going from the known to the unknown, we can believe that when we enter the larger life there will be loving hands to greet us and loving friends to care for us until we become accustomed to our new surroundings.

Dr. Ernest Holmes, author of *The Science of Mind*

DAD AND ME

My father made his transition several years ago. I'd always thought I would be involved in his final weeks, days, and hours. But he had another plan going for the final parting, one that took precedence not only over my being there but also over anybody's being there. He had always been in control of his life and his immediate surroundings, and I assume he didn't intend the termination of his life to be any different.

My sister and mother, who were both with him in the final days, told me the details and the unfolding, step-by-step drama of a failing ninety-year-old heart that had been previously battered and bruised and was just worn out.

Dad's will to live had been sliding away over the previous months. His naps got longer, food was less interesting to him, his world got smaller and smaller, and the least stress caused him chest pain. He suffered a heart attack at home, and though he'd said "no more hospitals, no heart surgery, no heroics," and all the correct legal papers to support those intentions were signed, when my mother said, "Let's go to the hospital. They'll stop your pain," he agreed and they went.

In the ER they medicated and tranquilized him, stopped his pain, and admitted him to the heart-care wing. There they hooked him up to their life-sustaining equipment, for they were going to stabilize and save him, this ninety-year-old heart patient. I know he knew better and only voiced strong objections when, to his disbelief and mine, heart surgery was suggested by a consulting doctor.

On his final evening, he asked to be unhooked, allowing him to sit alongside my mother on a small couch that was in the room. They touched and talked softly together. At one point, when he began to tire of sitting up, Mother said to him, "I wish I could take you home with me tonight." Then they kissed and he was helped into bed and hooked up for the night. Their final words were, "I'll see you in the morning. I love you."

In the middle of the night, when he was all by himself, he left. He left all things in his life in proper order—labeled, with full instructions—and he just quietly left . . . the way he always wanted to do it.

Over the previous five years, I had anticipated being the provider of emotional support for Dad. We'd made our peace—or at least I had healed my anger and resentment toward him—and now we were talking male to male as we grew older.

He maintained a very private and controlled emotional system, whereas I was open and exploring every possible avenue of insight. But at the very core of our beingness, we both shared the same patterning and value systems. We could talk and agree, or agree to disagree, with very few words because we started with the same core premise on almost all matters of conscience. It was nice to be understood at a soul-level by a parent, by my own father. I will always miss not having had those final days, hours, and minutes of his life-experience with him.

He had wisdom to be shared that he seldom let out, and I always will feel I didn't get enough of it from him. Maybe later, maybe there is more to come for me from him on the next plane.

A friend made this wonderful statement when his mother died: "I really wasn't through with her yet . . ." I have the same feeling about my father. *I really wasn't through with him yet . . . .*

Richard Robinson, RScP, *son.*

MY THOUGHTS ON BEING WITH DYING PEOPLE

The most important thing about being with people who (believe they) are dying is to be centered in one's knowingness that life is eternal—and at the same time to have a special reverence for the significant moment about to occur, much like one would have a special feeling for a wedding or a graduation ceremony.

Just like being with those who believe they are going to live for a while, an important key in successful relationships is to meet people where they are. In other words, I would not be with any two people in exactly the same way. It depends on many factors, including infirmities, intentions, timing, and soul growth.

Keep your own vibration high. That is a real key. It will provide the resonance to assist others to do what they really want to do—whatever that is.

And . . . help the other people choose to focus on what makes them feel good, without any avoidance at all. Begin with facilitating awareness, acceptance, and responsibility. Finally, move on to forgiveness and gratitude. Then the people can focus on what they enjoy and desire, and do so in a free and real way.

Dr. David Kamnitzer, *teacher, spiritual guide, therapeutic nutritionist.*

MOVING CONSCIOUSLY INTO THE MYSTERY

Chuck was dying of pancreatic cancer when Carolyn, a friend and mentor, came to visit. With Chuck's family gathered around, she asked him, "If you were to comment on what's happening to you, would you say you are moving toward life or toward death?" Carolyn, who is very intuitive, had told me earlier that she was certain Chuck was dying, yet in her wisdom she directed the question toward him, so he could reach deeply into his own soul to have the realization himself.

Chuck did not hesitate long. He said, "I think I am moving toward death."

Carolyn said, "I think you are too, and you have the rare opportunity of bringing consciousness to your dying." Chuck's two grown children, Carolyn, and I (his wife) formed a circle around his bed, and Carolyn asked us to express our feelings and then Chuck to express his. We each told him we were very, very sad, and also that we were respectfully aligned with his soul's journey. Chuck then gave each of us the personal gift of a final "message." The circle felt sacred; we were ritualizing his passage.

That evening, Chuck called us into his room and said, "I think I'm dying. What do you think?"

When I said to him, "Yes, Chuck, I think you are dying," he looked at me and said, "My God, you have courage."

And, indeed, in that moment of accepting the process of his dying, I was infused with a rush of energy which, until that moment, had been the energy of denial. There was an empowerment that came with the acceptance. And this is the message I have tried to convey to caregivers since Chuck's death.

Chuck and I experienced a deep cellular and soulful healing that happened when we accepted what Life offered, even though it was not our ego's preference. We were shown that there is a harmonious timing for dying as well as for living.

After the acceptance of his dying, Chuck himself seemed to be in a state of grace. He was taking heavy doses of morphine to try to alleviate an excruciating pain in his abdomen. Yet periodically from then on, he radiated a clarity which broke through the drugged and altered state of the morphine. Three days later, during his last hours, we spent several poignant hours holding hands around his bed. At one point he declared, "I'm ready." In the room, there was a sense of brilliance and joy.

I looked at his face and knew in my heart that his journey was exactly right, that we all were participating in a sacred transformative moment.

His last words were, "I see the trail up the mountain." We stayed with him in silence, occasionally speaking from the heart, "I love you," "You are on a sacred path," and "I'll hold you in my heart always." Eventually my daughter and I simultaneously let go of his hands, because we sensed the rest of his journey was to be solo. We all witnessed his face as it seemed to be working through some huge transition. Then he breathed his last breath, shortly after midday.

In the room for the rest of the afternoon, we sat in a state of reverence and extreme bliss. The room itself seemed buoyant. His body was no longer burdened. There was no emotion, but there was a pervading feeling of joy. We sat with hearts open. There was nothing to know, nothing to process. We seemed to be at a threshold between worlds. Chuck had left us at the gate and moved into the Mystery.

Virginia Fauvre, teacher and counselor.

THE HOLY PRIVILEGE

There are four profound universal mysteries: birth, initiation, marriage, and death. To be in the presence of any one of these mysteries is a holy privilege. It is a gift of deep spiritual remembrance and healing for all those who participate or are present at any one of these human mysteries.

Human beings world-wide have chosen to ritualize or ceremonialize each of these sacred transitions. Often, when we are present at an external event that marks a sacred transition, there is an internal process that is being simultaneously mirrored to the individuals involved. To be present or participate in any of these mysteries is considered "A Great Blessing" by many indigenous peoples of the world.

The following Inuit prayer states so eloquently why we must constantly open to the grace, love, respect, dignity, and wisdom that is prevalent for us at these special occasions:

Oh, mystery of mysteries, let me not forget who I am, and why I have come, and why I will go.

Let me open to all mysteries while I am on Mother Earth, so I can stay connected to the Sacred and all living creatures.

May we come humbly and respectfully to each of the mysteries we are invited into, for they reconnect us to the good, true, and beautiful in this great gift of *Life*.

Angeles Arrien, Ph.D., *cultural anthropologist, teacher, author.*

MOTHER'S FINAL YEARS

Mother lived seven years after Dad left her alone and frightened. I remember Dad's admonition in his own last years: "Take care of your mother." And though I heard it and received it clearly as a commandment, I did not realize the full extent of all this order to serve her would ultimately entail. She was so dependent on Dad for almost all decisions that after his death, she was "rudderless" and really wanted to leave this life also.

Her eyes had already begun to fail in her eighties, and now her lifelong pattern of depression was compounded by fear and doubt regarding whatever lay ahead for her—alone now. My sister and I tried daily in-home help, keeping her in her home, in the neighborhood, surrounded by friends and relatives.

This transition period was of short duration, since we knew a care facility with "assisted living" would be the next required move, and very soon. My sister and nephew scouted out a deluxe facility that met her immediate needs, where she could afford her own small apartment, have her medications supervised, and take meals either privately or communally. It was a very nice, senior care "resort" and she liked it—the services, the attention, and surprisingly, the community activities. Though I had been concerned about her adapting to the mixing and the interaction in this new community, she came alive again and was more social than I had ever seen either of my parents be before. She liked dressing up for dinner at night and going to afternoon lectures, book reviews, and the Happy Hour, with its wine and cheese (neither of which she had enjoyed before!).

A significant turnaround had taken place and for the next five years we all felt good about her future, as she had a very secure and comfortable lifestyle. But then gradually a downward spiral began—with a "little fall," a missed chair-seat, or tumbling to the floor as she bent over to retrieve something.

What had been "assisted living" care was no longer enough to help her in getting up, sitting down, or walking—even in the familiar spaces of her own apartment.

My sister, who lived a convenient twenty minutes away from Mother, now became the "911" source for help, for support and for connection.

The Adjacent Child Syndrome had set in. This means that regardless of the living circumstances and security that have been put in place, a call for help is made to the child who is geographically closest.

The calls to her from Mother often became irrational requests related to the smallest of needs, to something missing or misplaced, to the most trivial of dilemmas. Since my sister and Mother had never been on the best of terms anyway, this compounded tensions and evoked anger in both of them. We soon had a "moth-and-flame" situation—a push-and-pull of obligation, guilt, resentment, concern, and anger. It proved not to be "fixable," except for short periods on family-together occasions that we called "make-nice times."

I suggested that Mother change residences and move nearer to me. After some investigation at both locations and much discussion, Mother decided she could live better where she was—with the addition of a personal caregiver. We arranged for that to happen and soon had reached another plateau of care that stabilized her once again.

Her fears and doubts about everyday situations began to combine with her tendency toward depression, then dementia and paranoia started to show up. This often called for adjusting the meds, the caregivers, and their time with Mother, but still she felt she was "losing control of her life." And in truth she was, for her vitality was flowing gradually out of her body. There were more bad days than good days.

Things were now disappearing, being "taken from her." I saw this as symbolizing part of her inner work to stay in control, to hold on—and also as the beginning of her letting go. We were witnessing the inner dance of detachment, the dis-

solving of her soul into a time of gestation and birthing that
was about to come in her new life experience. It was her tug-
of-war, her indomitable perseverance as she sought to survive
all that she sensed was leaving her. It was her fear of the unknown.

By this time, I had become a licensed Religious Science
Practitioner, and I called on every skill I had acquired in my
training, every instinct I had honed, to bring reassurance to
Mother by realigning her with her Christian faith to relieve
her fears about what would happen to her next.

I set up Dad's photo for her, lighted his memorial candle,
put on a meditative music tape, and started affirmative visualizations, seeking to assure her that her journey was very
gently transitioning into a bigger, grander, more expanded
form of life, that Dad was already there to receive her and
hold her hand again, and that her faith in Jesus and his message was a guiding light into her next expression of Life. I
tried to bring about an opening in her awareness whereby she
might glimpse a parting of the veil, might perhaps dream one
night of Dad standing and awaiting her arrival. I also offered
intense and heartfelt spiritual mind treatments over her bed
on those final visits, but they were as much for me as they
were for her, since she was on her own spiritual pathway . . .

She continued on a downward spiral as, more and more,
her body systems shut down. She experienced many of the
preludes to passing that are in the legendary wisdom as well
as others to which her hospice nurses and her wonderful His-
panic caregivers had alerted us—the agitated nighttimes; the
middle-of-the-night "terrors"; the strong desire to be free of
all clothing and bed covers, including her diapers; her anger
at having to stay in bed at night, even though she could no
longer stand, walk, or even sit upright. We learned to leave a
low-wattage light on all night with instrumental music tapes
playing, for her greatest terror came in the quiet still and
darkness of those long nights.

Food became so unappealing that her consumption was down to nearly zero. Nothing sounded good to her. But just ten days before her transition, we asked her if she would like to go out to dinner and she said, "Yes!"

She didn't just say yes. She also got excited and involved in the who, when, and what-to-wear of the occasion. It was a very special event, and she not only rose up for it, but she took charge and orchestrated it as well, just the way she had done in the years since Dad left. She became the social Grande Dame for this one last time.

Then, on the morning of her ninety-fifth birthday, she took her final breath and left her tired, shriveled body behind.

We flew to Nebraska, taking her to the small farm-community cemetery where Dad had purchased plots and their headstones. Here with their two families, his and hers—those early pioneering families—she rests now alongside Dad.

I gave a brief service for some fifteen friends and the few of her family members who remain. We shared stories, in-sights, laughs, and tears. But living as Mother had—to ninety-five and dying on her ninety-fifth birthday, in her own bed, pain-free, and just worn-out—she had left us little to mourn. She had worn this life out, and it was time for her to move on, to leave that body behind.

Richard Robinson, RScP, *caregiver, son.*

FROM THE MOTHER OF UNITY

An excerpt from a letter to a grieving daughter, written in approximately 1926.

We are with you constantly, dear, to help you realize that all is well. Your dear one did not know how to let go of the limitations into which her mind had got, nor to renew and build up her body. So to her it is a rest, and an opportunity to lay aside the body for a time and to break the conscious connection with things going on around her, until the divine urge within her again prompts her to build the body temple and take up lessons here in the physical.

If your mother had gone away on a vacation and you knew she was in loving hands, you would not be grieved or worried, would you? Well now, that is just what has taken place. She is resting from the suffering and the problems that she did not know how to manage. She is in the presence of God just as you are; and the best way to show your love for her is to let go all human longing and all sense of loss, so that this soul who welcomed you as a babe, and who has cared for you, may rest assured all is well with you. Your mother has just gone onto a different schoolroom of life, where the divine Father-Mother is the teacher.

Myrtle Page Fillmore, "Mother of Unity," co-founder of Unity Church and Unity School of Christianity, Unity Village, Missouri.

THE HEALING CALLED FORGIVENESS

In her powerful work, Elisabeth Kubler-Ross often refers to the necessity of completing "unfinished business." I believe that high on the list of such matters is speaking one's true feelings to past and present relationship partners. For example, I remember the incredible sense of relief I felt when my ex-husband and I jointly agreed that each of us had done the very best we could in our marriage relationship—and we parted company as friends.

It also applies to one's parents. A few months ago, I knew nothing about the aging process, elder care, or caregiving for the dying. Now I do, for my mom is aging noticeably and needs considerable care. I'm experiencing the grief of losing her a bit at a time. For both of us, this is a time for speaking our true feelings, healing past woundings—and coming to the point of forgiveness. In my recent reading and research, I've noticed a continuous thread of advice about the process of—the need for—forgiveness, both of others and of oneself.

Many years ago in a class on fiscal responsibility, the instructor, Foster Hibbard, stressed the necessity for forgiveness of oneself as a key component for building wealth. That seemed strange. I should have thought learning about economics or the inner workings of the stock market was more important for building wealth. But he emphasized this teaching about *forgiveness*, even suggesting that we silently say to *every* person we meet, "I forgive you." This, he declared, is a powerful affirmation that opens doors and permits us, and those to whom we say it, a peaceful entry to wherever we're going. He believed our culture has so reinforced self-guilt that when we forgive others, we are giving permission to our psyche to forgive ourselves, also. Only then is there a release from suffering, pain, and sorrow.

The Unity philosophy teaches that we are One with all—with everything. We discover wisdom, then, in forgiving everyone, because in our *oneness* we are forgiving ourselves. All forgiveness is simply self-forgiveness. When we forgive ourselves, we end the cycle of draining energy into unfinished business, into guilt, shame, and "shoulds." Then, since nature abhors a vacuum, we find ourselves replacing the old, negative energy with Life's new, fulfilling flow of acceptance, abundance, and Love.

In practice, it takes courage. I know that. I am presently at a major turning point in my life. Everything I've loved, dreamed of, and strived for has temporarily crashed around me. The tendency to blame, criticize, and bludgeon myself feels overwhelming. My mind knows these thoughts and feelings are self-defeating and can *lock* me into a downward spiral of hopelessness and depression.

Charles Fillmore, co-founder of Unity, asserted, "Forgiveness is my daily business." He disciplined himself to review his day mentally just before sleep each night. He acknowledged himself for the positive outcomes that had come about; the actions he regretted, he mentally changed until they had a positive result. Each occasion of cross words, uncomplimentary thoughts, and hasty judgments was reviewed and revised. Norman Vincent Peale used this same method. He said it gave him the most peaceful sleep, and that he never needed to count sheep again!

In her book *How Did I Become My Parent's Parent?*, author Harriet Sarnoff Schiff suggests that we begin a *"forgiveness project*," taking time daily to list those occurrences, major and minor, that went astray or haywire and for which we blame ourselves for allowing to happen. This is a process of cleansing and clearing away of old stuff.

Try it! Make a *forgiveness list* of everything and everybody you need to release. Then start another list, a *gratitude list*, and every day write down from three to five things or people or events you are really thankful for which came into your life during that day. See where the sadness is for you, and see where the joy and Love and fullness are for you.

The point to realize is that resentment, guilt, and shame tie us in knots emotionally and physically and restrict us from having free choice—whether in quality living or quality in making a peaceful transition. Releasing these feelings can be a very cleansing process for a relationship, a group, or a family to use whenever change, separation, or transition is approaching. A wonderful affirmation for this is: I AM NOW FREE FROM ALL RESENTMENT OR ATTACHMENT TOWARD OR FROM PEOPLE, PLACES, OR THINGS OF THE PAST OR PRESENT. I AM NOW IN THE RIGHT PLACE WITH THE RIGHT PEOPLE FOR MY GROWTH, MY BLESSINGS, AND MY WHOLENESS.

Therese Godfrey, *Unity Teacher; Minister, Church of Practical Theology.*

We sometimes congratulate ourselves at the moment of waking from a troubled dream—it may be so the moment after death.

Nathaniel Hawthorne

LIFE MOVES ME FORWARD

The change people fear most is death, but this is a needless fear. We are God, wearing a garment of flesh. When we get through our time on Earth, we must shed this body because it is too gross to carry further. We have to drop it just like taking our clothes off. We came with nothing, and we leave with nothing.

I let life move me forward into greater joy. There are no anchors in my world to fasten me to any one situation. I accept the ever-changing, ever-unfolding action of God in my experience. I appreciate the past, but it cannot bind me to any person, place, or thing. These ideas will take me out of the present into the heaven of fresh conditions . . .

Nana Veary, RScP, *mystic, Hawaiian Lore teacher, and student of Christianity, Spiritualism, metaphysics, and Zen Buddhism.*

"IT WAS ALL WORTHWHILE . . ."

When I called Elisabeth Kubler-Ross and asked her to contribute to this book, she responded by saying she was incapacitated right now due to a recent stroke. But I took the following notes of wisdom from her tapes and lectures, and she agreed to release them for publication in this book.

I am grateful to Elisabeth for the teachings she has brought to me over the years. She has been a wayshower of compassion in action in this arena, and I know she has helped and guided many others who step forward to hold another's hand. I am indeed grateful.

Richard Robinson

As a student nurse is dying, she asks her caregivers to respond to her with human contact and compassionate care. "I know you feel insecure, don't know what to say, don't know what to do. But believe me, if you care, you can't go wrong. Just admit that you care. Don't run away; all I want to know is that there will be someone to hold my hand when I need it. I am afraid. Death may be routine to you here, but it is new to me. I have never died before and I am afraid . . . I wish we could talk; it wouldn't take much more of your time really. If only we could be honest together and admit our fears, maybe touch each other. If you really cared, and cried with me, would you really lose much of your valuable professionalism? Then it won't be so hard dying in this hospital with you as my friend close by . . ."

The most frightening aspect of our dying is fear of having to do it alone and also not having it take place surrounded by familiar possessions and things. Dying in a care facility, even the best, is not at all as comforting and reassuring as dying in one's home surrounded with those who you love and who love you. Hospitals' role of health care in society has changed, and they are no longer a place to go to die. They are fundamentally committed to healing, to curing, to restoring and the recovery process. In a hospice, a nursing home, or the patient's own home a more focused, loving, and compassionate care and staffing will be provided. Here the perceived "failure to cure or heal" the patient is not of any concern, where in the hospital it remains the institutional mandate. Death can then be prepared for in a peaceful and loving place.

Death is the final stage of our growth in life. There is no total death, as only the body dies here. The spirit or soul or whatever you may want to call it is eternal and moves on. And if we really want to live life we must have the courage to recognize and appreciate that life is very short and that everything we do counts here. Then when we face the evening hours of our lifetime, we will be able to look back and say, "It was all worthwhile because I have really lived."

Elisabeth Kubler-Ross, M.D., *psychiatrist, author, teacher.*

THE EDITOR'S APPRECIATION

As my publisher and I were wrapping up this book for its first printing—in fact, as the cover was being designed—word came to me that Elisabeth had made her transition, on the evening of August 24, 2004, at her home in Scottsdale, Arizona.

It was all worthwhile, Elisabeth! I am grateful for all you have taught us, given us to help ease the fears and anguish that surround this transition called death. I will miss your guiding light. I wish you *Godspeed* into your next Life.

MY OWN TRANSITION—CALLED DEATH

I have no worries or questions regarding an afterlife. I grew away from the old fear-based teachings about hell several years back, and I've often thought heaven may just be like the next big workshop—say "Life-II." In any case, whatever happens *then* will be part of the "package deal" that starts with my experiences *here* and *now*.

Occasionally in the past, when my circumstances were difficult, I even considered intentionally moving a little farther along my path by self-graduating myself into Life-II. This was not the result of morbid self-pity or a defeatist point of view. I simply pondered the possibility, looking at my options. I actually think this is common among those of us who work daily and deeply with patterns of pathos—our own and others'. It is something we must face directly and not bury psychologically.

I was sure that if I hurried along to the next workshop level—Life-II—it would bring new beginnings, with exciting material and fresh horizons. But then came my awareness that the concerns I wanted to detour around were mine to work on *here and now*, before I *could* graduate. This was reminiscent of my childhood training, from which I got a strong work-ethic, a dedication to responsibility and obligation: vegetables before dessert, homework before playtime, money-making before money-spending. Do the practical stuff first. I'm still that way, so that shortcut to Life-II, which might have seemed momentarily like a possibility for "escape," a safety valve, was not a real option for me.

Now I am *here*. I've been helped along by many teachers, teachings, therapies, and different kinds of reading. I love most of the life-experiences that come to me, and the ones I don't care so much for, I work with, searching for the "hidden pony inside" or stopping to take a view from another perspective. Looking at the whole, at the larger picture, often changes my perception and stops me from any rush-tojudgment. I am now fully aware that the *journey* holds the joy, the discovery, the thrill of life for me—whatever the destination may ultimately reveal. I am loving "Life-I" more each day.

When the time comes for my transition, for my departure from this level of existence, I hope I am fully attuned, connected with God, and aware that I am always on my pathway, on purpose, "named and present." And if my physical circumstances seem negative or are contrary to my hoped-for gentle release, I pray that someone is available to remind me, or is called forward, or just shows up to *hold my hand.*

My worries and concerns about my death seem trivial as I write about them—as if I were rearranging the deck chairs on the Titanic or worrying about a Sunday pot-roast dinner while all of Angola is starving. But these worries and concerns of mine are nevertheless *my real stuff,* related to unfinished business, unresolved issues, and feelings of not having completed all the work I would or could or should have done here.

My feeling about the separation of death now, in my sixties, is not the same as it was years ago, because family, lovers, and friends are leaving more frequently these days. My viewpoint, my perspective, shows me that we all enter in the middle of a movie and we leave a little further along, but still in the movie. I now see the Life Cycles, the continuum.

Back in the eighties, I learned in a Stewart Emery workshop about a historical circumstance in which people lived and died, then others came, lived, and died, and in that legacy generations came and passed—as they labored to build the Great Wall of China. Most of those people never experienced the completion of the Wall. That struck me to my core, for I know that I have issues of separation and unfinished business interwoven within me. Goal-attainment, achievement, accomplishment, and accountability are attributes I have seen as pleasing to God and that I brought to God in my work. Now I wondered whether all of that really matters. What if

God doesn't keep records of such stuff on me? Perhaps I had latched onto a Sunday-school teaching—of God keeping score. And so I let it go. I am beginning to lay my worries down. I can handle what I can handle, smooth out the way where I can. But some issues are beyond my helping hands. So I get out of the way and let God be God.

Undoubtedly the greatest fear I have about my death—should it happen right now—is this: did I make the most of my *life*? Am I doing and being all I can to fulfill my life's purpose of learning more about compassion, forgiveness, joy, thanksgiving, and service? I want to know I have lived 100% of my life's potential.

I always remember David Spangler's telling a large group at the Asilomar Conference Center that he felt he was "God's legs, feet, arms, and hands," that he "did the work of God." I was struck by that image and the shift necessary for me to consider it: that I must turn 180°—from facing the Sacred Center and bowing in adoration . . . to turning and becoming the *rays* of the Sacred Center, my legs and arms becoming extensions of the Sacred in service—doing this work. I learned that I was not so much needed in adoration and praise as I was needed in service. This was a very strong image shift for me.

Will I—can I—ever feel I have done enough in service for anybody or anything in need? *No.* It is, in fact, an unanswerable question for me. I am always hearing, in response, "How big is your God?" I remember a teaching about the limitless scope and vision of God-Potential, and I know that nothing but my own perception of limitation holds me back. God is out there being a "100%-full-volume God" all the time. So I won't have finished all my service projects and dreams when I make my transition, but I will be primed for the next level of service—*and for what is required of me then and there.*

Richard Robinson, RScP, *caregiver, student.*

LOOKING AT DEATH DIFFERENTLY

Today, I am willing to look at death differently.

Perhaps our biggest fear in life has been death because we have mistakenly believed that our only identity was limited to the body. Let us be willing to look at death differently, remembering that 'I am not a body. I am still as God created me.'

Let us remind ourselves that as God's Creations of Love, we are everlasting, never-ending, and eternal. Let us strive to remember that life and the body are not the same; hence, there need be no fear when the body is put to rest.

Gerald Jampolsky, M.D., and Diane Cirincione are authors, teachers, and lecturers. Dr. Jampolsky is founder of the Center for Attitudinal Healing.

"MUY MISTERIOSO"

Death was never a stranger to me. The process of dying, the funeral service, and the proper period of mourning were all rituals held in high esteem and respected by my family.

One of my first memories was of my grandmother's death and funeral, and the "death watch" that preceded it. It was all explained to me by my Aunt Olivia that night, about how she was going to leave and go to heaven. Heaven sounded like a nice place to go, although it seemed quite mysterious to me and still does. A lot of my questions went unanswered at the time and still do.

My mother was never afraid of death and never understood anyone who professed any fears of it. She had been deprived of her parents at a very young age and had always felt there was something missing because they left her so soon. When she found out that she was dying, she had a few regrets about some things in the future, but didn't mind leaving because she was sure she would be reunited with them and somehow complete that cycle.

I was with her when she made her transition, and I tried to help her as much as I could with visualizations and with letting go of what few ties she had to this Earth. It was the first time I had actually been present when anyone left, and I was amazed at how simple and peaceful it was.

An "angel" named Helen who had been living with and helping my mother was the only other person with me. I looked at Helen and asked, "Is that it?" Helen who had been a witness countless times before said, "That's it."

Death is a very simple process. The events leading up to it may be dramatic due to a prolonged illness or unresolved problems or unsaid feelings, but the actual moment of transition takes as long as a sneeze. Still *muy misterioso*.

Fred Wiedenbeck, *student.*

When you love someone, it means you want them to go where they will be happiest, even if that means leaving you . . .

Unknown

PRACTICES FOR LIVING AND DYING

Things which matter most
must never be at the mercy of
things which matter least.
—Johann Wolfgang von Goethe

I don't know about death because I am among the living. Ah! I know something about death because I am among the living. As I awaken to the wholeness of life, I turn toward what matters most. When I imagine what my last words might be, I am brought back to what matters most in life as the cycle completes itself.

It has been said that we die the way we are born. Imagine the blessings that come with each birth. Imagine each being brought into this world blessed with life, each mountain meadow blessed with early morning dew born into the midday sun, each moment born into the next moment. Birth also blesses us with teachings about the cycle of life and death. Birth contains the essence of freshness and purity, of unlimited possibility, of the true ground of being as well as its own eventual end.

Like fine French wine, which reveals—through its taste—the essence of the soil where it was grown and the quality of the sunlight in its vineyard, we may sense the mystery that reveals our origins. Death is each moment yielding to the next, each drop of rain yielding to the next, each sunrise yielding to each sunset. Just as each moment is blessed with the potential for another birth, each life yields to the next in an endless cycle of love and blessing. Death reminds us of our origins as a natural part of the cycle just as life reminds us of our origins. So each moment is a fresh ground of living and dying dissolving back into the unknown.

Life and death bring us closer to our own authentic ground of being and closer to what matters most. In right relationship to life and death, we embody what matters most—

so practice with all your heart and soul. Practice being aware in every moment of the beauty, blessing, tragedy, and terror in life and death. As Rilke says, ". . . for beauty's nothing but the beginning of terror we're still just able to bear . . ."

Practice knowing that it's not what you think. We think we know and we know we think, meanwhile beauty is all around us, unnoticed by our own certainty. Can we see the beauty and blessing in everything that life and death have to offer? The dirty dishes in the kitchen aren't what we think; they're a sign of a well-lived life. The hurt feelings aren't what we think; they're a sign of a small place in need of expansive love.

Practice wisdom sensing the vast dimension of the source of our being where certainty doesn't exist. My third-grade teacher opened me to a perspective that has stayed with me all my life, though I have forgotten it many times. She pointed out the window to a baseball game and asked, "If the Martians came from space, how would they explain this event?" Wisdom comes in the most ordinary way to grace us with innate peace and knowing far beyond our thinking dimension.

Practice living the title of your first book. Everyone is a book waiting to be written. The current title of my book is *It's Okay Sweetheart*, a tale of agony and ecstasy with a surprise ending (it's not what I thought). It opens my heart to the wonder of relationship of the good, the bad, and the ugly in my life, and I feel all's right with the world.

Live your life as if it were a book containing a large dose of gratitude mingled with the agony and the ecstasy of your life. Like all good novels, every nuance and twist and turn in life weaves the fabric of a life wholly and uniquely ours. Practice feeling the grace of realizing that our humanity is more precious than perfection. Our humanity is perfection as it is and reminds us of the wholeness of our being. Practice feeling inspiration; be aware of what opens your heart and inspires your soul, for this is the natural blessing and liberation arising from the depths of your own being.

Practice your last words. Practice what you would say just before the moment of your death. My last words with gratitude—"there was no other way"—embody for me the absolute surrender and acceptance of the totality of my life and death. Those same words bring me closer to my true aliveness.

Gently remind yourself of the depth of your being and greet your joys and pains with the same hospitality you would offer to the stranger at the door. Remember the inspiration of a lifetime that's been forgotten and let it infuse your being with a sense of the sweetness in both living and dying.

As a high school student, I was moved by General McArthur's credo, *Live with Enthusiasm*, and I carry it in my wallet to this day, frayed and torn like a well-lived life. In part, it says, "so long as your heart receives messages of beauty, cheer, courage and grandeur and power from the earth, from man and from the Infinite, so long are you young."

Practice your last words as if you would live forever with enthusiasm and gratitude.

At the eleventh hour there is surrender
there is the door waiting only for you to walk through
will you love to live again
Beloved at the abyss, to love and be loved
Lava Hot Springs, Idaho
May 28, 1996

Linda Anderson

ELDERS' CARE AND GENTLE RELEASE

Holding the aged, tired, wrinkled hands of elders as they prepare for their final days here and their ultimate transition was not something I had experienced in the early stages of this book project. As I mentioned earlier ("Dad and Me," p. 11), I expected my father's final care to be my responsibility and my first experience with a true elder. He, however, elected to go out quietly, fully in control, on his own timing—and alone. Then seven years later I had the opportunity and privilege of holding my mother's hand as she got ready to leave her body at age ninety-five ("Mother's Final Years," p. 17). So even as this book was being compiled, I gained the personal insight that was necessary for me to add my contribution to what's offered here.

I want to recommend a prerequisite: that you have, as much as possible, already examined and worked with your own needs for self-healing. You, as caregiver, must know your connection to Spirit if you are to be at peace as you are faced with the care of a parent or any immediate family elder. This most sacred time of being with a parent, spouse, or sibling in their final days/hours is not a time to release any anger onto them or onto Spirit. This is not meant to imply that family healings can't happen or shouldn't be attempted, but their gentle release from this space and time, I pray, will be peaceful and calm, and may include forgivingness on everybody's part, starting with you, the caregiver. Don't work it. Let the energy flow of its own accord; there are no "correct" ways to end life here. A process is underway already.

I believe this special time for closeness, healing, closure, and passing the wisdom forward can be made as quiet, serene, peace-full, and also joy-full as each of us as caregivers can envision for ourselves. After the legal necessities are handled and in place for those obligations (and I choose not to go into those here, since many books, articles, and services give this type of aid now), after the required "stuff" is put out of the way, our responsibility and duty, I believe, is to see that all the comforts—the release from anxieties, doubts, and fears—are handled in a one-on-one, very personal manner.

A dying friend once told me in his final days that although everything seemed okay and complete for him, his pet's planned care and security still didn't "sit well" with him. We reworked those arrangements until he could go on, feeling complete and at peace with the life his pet would have without him.

Often these little details (little to us) are rattling around as "worries" that cause anxiety to build. The little one-on-one talks often open both of us up to larger areas or perplexing quandaries as time appears to be running down. What "special giftings" or special private meetings would they like to have happen with their family and/or friends? As the caregiver, I know that I often become their rabbi, priest, minister, or spiritual practitioner, not so much for the final sacred rites and rituals, although that may happen too, but for those more mundane matters or questions that just pop out. What to wear, how hair and makeup should be, obituary wording, what music, what flowers?—all may become very important or not be important at all.

As the caregiver I ask what aromas, what music, what videos or opera tapes/CDs or recorded jazz concerts will bring back fond memories of the good times? What special foods or bakery goodies will bring cheer and joy into their life today? How can I help bring a calm serenity into this place at this time? You can hardly top having home-baked bread or chocolate chip cookies fill the room or the house with their smells!

And what about full-fragrance flowers, "jolts of joy" like tuberose, gardenias, night-blooming jasmine, lilacs, or old-fashioned home-grown roses? And if there are photos, art, "family treasures," trophies, or sacred talismans that remind the person of connections here, suggest that these be brought into the surrounding space. I believe all the senses need to experience the full rapture of joy—whatever that means and entails for the person at this time. Some may want to be read to or listened to as they tell their biography again. Others may just want quiet, serenity, and someone holding their hand.

Former First Lady Rosalynn Carter heads up an organization called "Last Acts," a group of care/support people dealing with the quality of life at the very end of this lifetime. Much help is showing up now in senior care hospice and palliative care to make one's final days/hours/minutes richer and more compassionate. We owe so much in this arena to Elisabeth Kubler-Ross, who taught and wrote about living a quality life until the very end. She has suggested that it may be an opportune time for sharing wisdom and insights between a dying person and family or friends, allowing the individual to become a "counselor" about death, about the particular life-threatening situation or dis-ease, about the coping techniques he or she uses. These are empowering possibilities, which give lasting meaning to the person's life and to his or her nobility.

In my own recent circumstances with my mother (who lived to her ninety-fifth birthday), my sister and I kept all the accoutrements and amenities from her lifetime collection around her in her final years . . . and final days. The Christmas tree, as well as other holiday and seasonal "chachkas" she always used and cherished, along with the photo albums and the picture-gallery wall, were surrounding her with family memories. We kept her in phone connection to her sisters and brother up until her final hours. Our intention was that she be comforted to the very end by these elements—the things of this lifetime, her home, and her family—that she had so cherished over those many years.

In my reading, I have found other little gems of insight into senior care and hospice service that I pass along here:

◊ Some people will already have had "glimpses beyond"—
an ever-so-brief parting of the veil or lifting of a curtain, a
view into their next life. Some, however, are going to
leave as "nonbelievers" in anything to come.

◊ Some will leave in pain, discomfort, or anxiety, no matter
how good and gentle your care for them has been. Others
will easily just "slip away."

◊ Some leave in the "Illusion of Dementia," often revealing
and releasing fears, doubts, and prejudiced beliefs of their
past. Perhaps only a word or a disjointed phrase is given
forth, but a caregiver should not discount or misjudge its
importance. I frequently felt these individuals were giving me gems and gifts out of the ether *or* from the depths
of their soul.

◊ Some will want to just "slip away," while others may
want loved ones—family and friends—around them near
the end. As I noted earlier, I called all of my mother's
friends and relatives in her final days, allowing each to
talk with her, to sit with her, and to bring flowers and
gifts while she was conscious, alert, and able to receive
their love.

◊ Some appear complete with their work here and ready for
the next plane—whatever that may look like. Others,
however, are not "okay" or ready to depart this lifetime,
which brings forth sadness for me even in my most compassionate caregiver role.

◊ Some, in their final days and hours, will be grateful to
you and forgiving of family and friends.

◊ Some will not be grateful or forgiving at all.

To me as a caregiver, any or all of these attitudes and
perspectives are just fine—appropriate and individualized to
the person who is leaving—for I know each of us will have
our own way, our own time, and *our own date to face our
transition.*

For us as caregivers, this pathway of service in palliative care is our sacred and privileged time of learning more about our own forthcoming transition process. And my heartfelt desire for each of us, when our time comes near, is that we find the warmth and gentle comfort of another's hand.

Richard Robinson, RScP, *caregiver, student.*

THAT WHICH IS ETERNAL WITHIN US

To be able to live fully, we must somehow come to terms with death, especially our fear of it. As a hospice social worker and human being, I've found that our most common fears include concern about not being able to bear the accompanying physical pain; fear of the "unknown"; fear of ceasing to exist after death; fear associated with being separated from loved ones; and fear of hell, usually of the eternal fire-and-brimstone variety that was instilled in many of us by early religious training.

Where is the way out of this literal "dead end" that the fear of death locks us into? Some would answer that the "way out" is the "way in"—that we can actually "dis-cover" something within us whose existence is independent of the physical body, brain, and limited ego-personality.

This "something" is the direct experience of our soul. Wisdom teachings from time immemorial counsel us to "go within" to discover the existence of the soul for ourselves— what Socrates refers to in the dictum "Know Thyself." With the help of a genuine spiritual guide, we can prepare for a healing passage by learning how to meditate on that which is eternal within us—the same Inner Light and Celestial Sound we experience at the time of death. To have an ongoing experience of ourselves on the level of soul is not only the best way that I know to prepare for our own death *during* life, but this state of awareness also helps us to be of better service at the bedside of those making the transition before we do. For when we finally know—from direct experience—that the Circle of Life is not broken at the time of physical dissolution, then we become liberated from the subliminal fear of death that has been insidiously robbing us of our life-energy during many of our years on this Earth.

Freed now from the fear of death, we will increasingly experience the transcendent, eternal love of the soul and of God—a Love that never dies.

Freed now from the fear of death, we will see beyond and through the perception-blinding prison of the shadowy past.

Freed now from the fear of death, we will discover an unlimited source of mercy within us. We will be able to truly forgive ourselves and others.

Freed from the fear of death, we will now have the courage not only to die, but also to really live for the first time.

Eliot Jay Rosen, *author, teacher.*

FLOW

Be
as water is,
without friction.

Flow around the edges
of those within your path.
Surround within your ever-moving depths
those who come to rest there—
enfold them,
while never for a moment holding on.

Accept whatever distance
others are moved within your flow.
Be with them gently
as far as they allow your strength to take them,
and fill with your own being
the remaining space when they are left behind.

When dropping down life's rapids,
froth and bubble into fragments if you must,
knowing that the one of you now many
will just as many times be one again.

And when you've gone as far as you can go,
quietly await your next beginning.

Noel McInnis, Minister, Church of Religious Science.

("Flow" appears again in the back of this book on page 119.
Readers are invited to cut that page out, photocopy it if they
wish, and share it freely with others.)

Death is just the final stage of our growth in this life . . .
The self or spirit, or whatever name you may wish to call it,
is eternal.

Elisabeth Kubler-Ross

TO BE IN SERVICE

It is easier to do than to talk or write about. Being in service is easier for me than writing about all it means to me. And the hardest lesson for me is to be still and know that all is well, while all around me I see people in need and others who are not seeing the need.

To be in service to others while I'm here seems to me to be my birthright, a reason to be that walks hand-in-hand with my learning all about "Life-I." I don't view service as a one-sided relationship.

In their wonderful book *How Can I Help?—Stories and Reflections on Service*, Ram Dass and Paul Gorman note that the title they chose, *How Can I Help?*, reflects "a timeless inquiry of the heart." They continue, "Yet we often hear it asked in the context of our own culture and moment. As commitment to service has ebbed and flowed, many of us have spent a great deal of time considering the deeper values of our helping work. What exactly is the nature of conscious service?"

For some, every possible way of being in service to others is a common, natural occurrence. For many, service is an open heart with simple gestures or expressions of kindness toward neighbors, friends, or even unknown "strangers." For others these days, giving money, writing checks, and making donations takes the place of human contact.

Throughout the pages of this book, you are being given shimmering glimpses of how others have been of service to parents, lovers, wives, husbands, other family members, friends, and some unknown "strangers" who were facing or had faced that peak moment of their transition from this life.

My most sincere hope and wish is that you be touched deeply by these stories, that the possibility of being able to *hold another's hand* comes to you and, in turn, someone will be there for you, also.

As Stewart Emery says in his brilliant "Quantum et Solace" (see p. 111), to make a commitment to be in service to all fellow living beings is "an enormous commitment . . ." To discover the fullness of what it means to be truly *human* and fully alive and "on purpose" is what *being in service* means to me.

In his book *Your Sacred Self*, Wayne Dyer makes three very direct and impactful statements that I have his permission to use here. They will give us wisdom to think on:

> Each day make an attempt to serve others in some small way and do not tell anyone. Slowly, the questions about your own value and why you are here will evaporate. Just one small extension of help or love to another, with no thought of what is owed back to you, will put you on the path of higher awareness.

> Copy this ancient truth and re-read it daily: "When you seek happiness for yourself it will always elude you. When you seek happiness for others you will find it yourself."

> Remind yourself every day that the highest worship of God is service to mankind and that it is through those acts that your sacred self will be realized. You do not need to convince others or yourself that you are divine. Do it in deed. Your inner awakening of joy and bliss will be reward enough.

When words of wisdom like these from Wayne Dyer, Stewart Emery, and Ram Dass stir our minds and hearts, we just need to ponder them—without judging what we did or didn't do before, or what didn't work right the last time. Just reflect on these thoughts.

Empathy and compassionate care, and the loving touch of our hands—those can be our most healing gifts.

Richard Robinson, RScP, *caregiver, student.*

SHARING
RECOLLECTIONS

In the Buddhist teachings, Avalokiteshvara, the Buddha of Compassion, is depicted as having a thousand eyes in order to see all the pain and suffering of the universe and a thousand arms to reach out and offer helping support and comforting.

SHARING RECOLLECTIONS

THE AIDS QUILT

I shall always remember the first AIDS March in Washington, D.C., in 1987, and day of the unfolding of the Quilt. I was one of many standing in line to read from a list of the names of people being honored who had died of AIDS and had a quilt panel made for them.

Just as it was almost my turn at the microphone, there was a tap on my shoulder and I turned around. A young man saw my name tag, screamed my name out loud, and flung himself in my arms, sobbing hysterically. Between his sobs he told me that his lover has been a fan of mine. As he lay dying, the last thing he asked for was that he be read to from one of my books. He left the planet listening to my words.

After I heard this story, I gently asked the young man why he had tapped me on the shoulder, for after all he did not know who I was at the time. He told me he had not had time to make a quilt, but he wanted his lover's name recited with all the others who died so tragically. The synchronicity was amazing. Of course I squeezed in his lover's name as I read from my list.

Tears still come to my eyes when I think of this special time. I shall always remember it.

Louise L. Hay, teacher, author, lecturer, publisher.

A CONVINCING SIGN

My belief in an afterlife was admittedly a bit tenuous. Stories of mysterious visits by butterflies and birds interpreted as communications from a deceased loved one were a little too coincidental for me.

My friend Marty, however, liked to paint life with bold strokes. Marty was dying of AIDS. He also suffered from Lazarus Syndrome. One day I would say my final goodbye as he lay semiconscious in a hospital bed; the next day he would yell "hello" as he sped by in his Land Rover.

"Don't you think you're pushing this resurrection thing?" I would tease.

Marty and I often discussed our beliefs about death. The last time his zestful energy seemed to be ebbing we jokingly talked about what "sign" he would use to convince me that he had survived the loss of his body. Always the trickster, Marty promised to "zap" me in a way that would leave no doubt.

A week after his memorial service I was sitting comfortably in my living room reading. Suddenly a bolt of electrifying energy shot through my body and lifted me to my feet. I cursed him, of course, then howled with laughter and relief.

Buz Hermes, *teacher, counselor, former Program Coordinator for Caregivers Support at KAIROS, San Francisco.*

A LETTER FROM A GOOD FRIEND

Dear Friends,
This letter is to inform you that David died very peacefully on Wednesday.

I saw David three times the day before he died, each time telling him how much I loved and respected him and how much I supported him completing this process however he chose.

Even though he hadn't been able to respond for several days, I knew that on some level he could hear me.

Several times I told him, "David, one thing I know for certain. When you are ready to go, you will go and it won't matter what medication you are on or not on at that time. I know you. Once you've made up your mind to do something, it's done! I trust you in this process."

He always smiled.

The hospital staff gave a prognosis of one to six months. As was to be expected, David did it just the way he wanted—with an element of surprise (some things never change!).

The evening he died, he had a two-hour visit from an old friend.

Meanwhile, I was across town singing "Remember Me" at the memorial service of a good friend of ours named Alex. At the end of the song, I asked Alex to help David let go whenever he was ready.

Sometime in the space between the end of David's friend's visit and my arrival later, David did let go.

Our friend Eileen joined me and we stayed as long as possible. The look on David's face was so peaceful. We had been telling him for several weeks that it was okay to let go. I like the image that Alex

*came to David from the other side and said, "It's
okay. Let's go!" and that's what David did.*

*David also requested that everyone be told that he
died of complications from AIDS. We must all do our
part to end this terrible disease. Awareness is the first
step. Please help us.*

Jerry

Gerald Wayne Florence, *songwriter, songmeister, minister of
music, and producer/publisher of New Thought spiritual music.*

(Editor's note: My friend Jerry joined Alex and David just
fourteen months later.)

Through hundreds of experiences I have realized it is the very same healing energy you send to someone to get well, as it is to die well—so there is no conflict. You don't have to be manipulating anything, you just send this great loving calm. And if the person is choosing to get well, it helps them to get well and if the person is not going to get well, it helps them to die well. It is just a great calm love, *an immense heart-filled calm love* . . .

Patricia Sun

A VALENTINE TO REMEMBER

Her real name was Ballentine. Yet when I first asked her name, I heard a "V" instead of the "B," so this wonderful name Valentine and an unforgettable nocturnal friendship were birthed in a hushed, darkened hospital corridor in the early morning of a spring day in 1974. The lilting, soft, sing-song Jamaican accent further enchanted me as she continued mopping the floor. She was striking in an ethereal sort of way—tall and lean, with temples silvered and her remaining short hair very black to match her eyes, all enhanced by a carriage suggestive of ancient nobility.

"Why do you want to know my name?" she inquired as she lowered her eyelids, looking down and away from me.

"Because of what happened in room 405," I said pointedly.

Just minutes earlier, I had finished evaluating a patient who was admitted to 405 with painful pleuritic chest pain. Returning to the nursing station, I began writing the orders for medications I felt would help her. "A strong analgesic," I thought, "and a muscle relaxant. A sleeping pill should she require it, chest x-rays, electrocardiogram. . . ."

As I was writing, I first glimpsed Valentine and her mop in her slow, rhythmic dance, moving from room to room down the hall. I thought I could even hear her humming softly—like a lullaby or a child's sweet song. She entered room 405.

I continued writing: "Aspirin for light pain, regular diet, vital signs every two hours until stable . . . ." I suddenly remembered that I had not asked my patient about any allergic reactions to medications she might have had. I started to enter her room, only to bump gently into Valentine. She graciously nodded her head and revealed a most wonderful smile. She was singing softly, I thought.

I entered 405, filled with physician responsibility. What I encountered greatly impacted me. My patient was sitting up in bed, relaxed, humming the same tune Valentine was singing.

"What's happened to you?" I asked. There was almost a tinge of attack in my voice.

"Oh . . . that wonderful woman came into my room to mop the floor. She was singing this childlike song."

"Did she say anything or do anything?" I probed.

"No. She just kept singing softly and mopping." My patient added, "I do feel much better, Dr. Joy."

A little deflated, I inquired about her allergies and left the room.

Which brings me to where I can finish this story.

"What happened in 405?" Valentine softly asked.

"The patient there is much better because you came into her room . . . that's what," I responded.

"I am very happy she is better. Yes, I am very happy she is better," was Valentine's response as she moved past me to get on with her work. I suddenly realized I was making her uncomfortable with such directness.

Through quiet hellos and eye embraces, our friendship initially deepened. Then one night she opened to reveal how Spirit had Called her. She had experienced the Healing Presence since childhood. Pets, people, and plants seemed to get better when she was with them. She called it "Spirit doings." I'll never forget her words: "Oh, I could never learn what you know to help the sick, Dr. Joy. So I prayed and prayed and Spirit said, 'Go be a night janitor in a hospital.' So here I am . . . still mopping, thirty-five years later!" She laughed. We both laughed. I, being 35, at myself. She, in childlike wonderment.

She had deepened my realization that something was missing in my soul training. Two months later my Call came in a loud inner voice that said, "Your life as a physician is over." The exploration of dreams that ensued began my apprenticeship as a night janitor to the soul.

W. Brugh Joy, M.D., *life-teacher and facilitator of spiritual transformation, author.*

THE EDITOR'S APPRECIATION

A student of Brugh's since 1987, I've often witnessed his great humility as a participant in this thing called Life—this great Mystery. His willingness to learn from what Life puts before him is his teaching. Brugh has taught me to look through the many facets of "reality," past those external experiences, to see beyond, to see more, and then to suspend judgments and appreciate the wonderment, the mysteries.

Ballentine's gift to the doctor carries an immense message—to see through the illusion of separation between us all, whether that of teacher/student, priest-priestess/disciple, or doctor/patient.

Brugh Joy is an inspiring teacher for me and for many . . . I appreciate his wisdom. I honor his soul.

Richard Robinson, *student.*

OPPOSITES IN HARMONY

More than twenty-five years after our divorce, Raymond, the father of my three daughters, was told he was dying of liver cancer. Karina, our oldest daughter, called from Nepal and told me she was feeling that she must come and be with her father. She further asked if she could bring him to Phoenix (where I live) and engage my assistance to see him, herself, and our other daughters through this transition.

Six months earlier, I had been told inwardly to set aside five weeks to begin writing a book. In addition, I had planned to devote two weeks to silence and fasting prior to a twelve-day residential seminar I was leading, named "Focusing on Heart Centering." As the fates would have it, I was now being asked to set aside my internal conflicts as well as having to forego writing my book. Nevertheless, time has a way of teaching surrender. Slowly, I set the unresolved feelings and protesting voices aside and opened my heart and my home.

As the days passed, the container opened and expanded so I could glimpse the quality of Raymond's soul, the difficulties he encountered, and his coping mechanisms. The tensions he and I had held during our adult lives gradually began to give way to the opening of our hearts—fully, unconditionally—giving way to the greatest healing of all, *the capacity of opposites to be together in harmony without opposition.* Simultaneously, this sacred time was also providing the space for the tension within him to transform into peaceful and blissful transition. He died a few days before I was to begin my twelve-day residential seminar.

Those seven weeks had been an unexpected gift. A deepening of the mysteries of life and death had occurred. I am extremely grateful for the forces that orchestrated the time and space so I would have the privilege of assisting in the most important journey of all—the journey back to God for which all life is a preparation.

Raymond and I had participated unconsciously and, most of the time, unwillingly in some of life's most awesome mysteries—the sacrament of marriage, the birth of three beautiful daughters, and the dissolution of the marriage. How inspirational, after more than a quarter of a century, that he initiated the four of us into the rituals of death. Each of our individual paths opened immensely to the mantle of life, embroidered with added dimensions of compassion, clarity, understanding, and acceptance.

As we celebrate the gift of life, the images we shared radiate with newfound levels of meaning. One cannot truly live until death has been befriended. Life is permanently embedded within all of us, never to be taken for granted again, adding an exciting edge every day upon our awakening. I often hear the words "If not now, when?" And off we go into a fuller incarnation.

Maria Elena Cairo, transpersonal teacher.

A DAUGHTER'S LOVING REMEMBRANCE

During surgery at age nine, my mother had a near-death experience. She spoke of floating above her body, of great peace, of light and not wanting to return. It sounded mysterious and Holy and very wonderful to me.

A widow for twenty-four years, my mother—Alta Mary Weir—was a tiny, beautiful woman who loved animals, enjoyed food and social events, and liked to travel. She was intuitive, with a remarkable sense of humor.

During her ninety-first year, Mother spoke of her two deceased sisters coming to see her during early mornings. Sometimes they stood at the foot of her bed or sat beside her. No words were spoken, just visits. I asked if she was dreaming and Mother's response was, "No, not at all."

We often spoke of death and I shared my understanding with her, saying, "It would be like taking off a heavy, worn-out coat and walking into another room, a room filled with light, peace, and love."

On her ninety-second birthday, August 30, 1996, Mother passed over and I was holding her hand as she struggled to breathe. During this period I gently urged her to let go, reminding her that the Angels were present and ready to take her into the Light.

It was a heart-wrenching yet wonderful experience for me. I was and I continue to be in awe of it all. Grieving is a process, a natural, necessary path toward wholeness. That's what I'm presently about—grieving, laughing, healing, and contemplating the light.

Elisabeth Flemmer

SOULS AT PLAY

A wonderful Quaker lady from Cambridge, in her sixties, was dying of cancer. I had never met her before but I was told that she wanted me to visit her. When we were alone in the room, she whispered, "Can you hurry this thing up? I'm bored."

I reflected on that opening gambit. Then I said, "You're probably bored because you're so busy dying all the time. Couldn't you die, say, ten minutes an hour, and do something else the rest of the time?" She smiled in understanding.

Then we did a meditation together, in which we listened to all the sounds around us—the children playing in the yard, the clock ticking on the mantle, the planes flying overhead. We felt the breeze on our faces, and the softness of the counterpane on the bed.

The drama of dying faded. Our Souls were at play together in the fields of the Lord, and we were in ecstasy together. She told me I could go, and she died peacefully a few hours later.

Ram Dass, *teacher, lecturer, author.*

TRIBUTE TO DEATH AND LIFE

"Mommy," she asked in a tear-crackled voice, "why doesn't Billy come to his window anymore?" Her query went unanswered. She rested her chin on the window ledge in despair. Another day was passing without her seeing his sparkling face, the one that lit up her world and dared her to laugh again. Though she knew he never left his apartment, she stretched to her toes to see the cobblestone street far below, hoping for a sign of him there. Alas, the familiar lonely feeling that had been her companion before finding Billy began creeping back. She even wondered if Billy's friendship was too good to be true.

Overwhelmed by the experiences of fleeing her war-ravaged homeland with her family, she was left bewildered and shy. Then, shortly after they settled in a quaint little German village, she first discovered that radiant face in the window across the street, and her life began anew.

Little Billy was hard to miss. His bright red hair circled his freckled face. Like morning sunshine, his glowing grin melted away the painful memories of her recent experiences. Those frightening pictures that flashed through her mind were now tucked away into some inner album during their playtime.

They had captured each other at first glance with the enchanting bond of childhood. Their only contact was from their facing windows, yet their hearts became linked by unconditional love, a love that's best understood by children.

Then a rope had been strung to connect the two windows, from which they exchanged notes and toys. Time and space melted away with puppet shows, peek-a-boo games, and bean-bag tosses. Passersby on the street far below were pelted on occasion from "invisible" sources. Magic was in the air again. Their hearts were filled with the miracle of living life free of fear, pain, or future uncertainty. In their innocence, they proved that not even war has the power to kill the spirit.

That imaginary album, a gift from Billy, existed in a place apart from time and space. Its inexplicable content could do no harm while it was closed and locked. Silently, amid their laughter and play, those terrifying memories slipped one by one from her mind and onto those sealed pages.

Mercifully, the treacherous picture book remained sealed for decades. Each page held a different memory. On one page was the picture of sitting with her family in silent fear through the long dark hours of the night. They were huddled around a huge radio waiting for the "voice," followed by sirens, warning them to return to the bomb shelter.

Mommy's beautiful eyes, distorted by fear and pain, stared from another page. Those pleading eyes asked what no one could answer: "How many more times must we leave behind everything we own?" There was Daddy's face, filled with rage and lined with worry. He did not tolerate the feeling of helplessness well. Big Sister wore a devastated expression. At nine years of age, she was taken to live in a sanitarium until she was healed of her contagious cough.

These and many more pages would be dealt with in the future. But for now, Billy was helping to build a sanctuary that would protect her for decades.

Time passed before she turned from the window. She chose not to disturb Mommy, who was busy at the sewing machine. The excitement of wearing the new outfit Mommy was hurriedly making distracted her from longing to see Billy. Very soon, she and Mommy would be going on a special outing. Anticipation opened the floodgates of excitement and other strange, new, out-of-control feelings.

Fear no longer dominated the family's surface lives, and the focus on mere survival was subsiding. New beginnings required new tools and the ability to readjust. Now they were safe, but they were strangers, foreigners. Knowing how to act in the new environment was confusing, and the little girl was clumsy, often stumbling over her desperate need to matter. Childhood had been on hold too long and it yearned to be reawakened and expressed.

Typical of a five-year-old, her impatience mounted until finally the day arrived to dress up in her new outfit. The stored energy was ready to burst from her little body like those exploding bombs in her homeland. Her hand in Mommy's hand, just the two of them all dressed up, they headed toward their adventure. She felt so pretty and proud on this very special day.

A favorite game to amuse herself was to skip on the raised stones of the cobblestone street, yet she resisted the temptation to show Mommy how clever she was at her game. She felt so stunning and proud in her new black jacket and matching skirt. Now and then her tilted face would touch the velvet collar of the bolero.

The feel of it brought up warm memories of when Mommy or once in a while Daddy or even the soldiers would rub her soft cheeks—or cold memories of the touch of the "bad" men. But the temptation to twirl in her full-circle skirt took over. The skirt danced around her waist. Joyfully she twirled and twirled and twirled, secretly hoping to be noticed.

Suddenly, she was jolted out of her ecstasy by the jerk of Mommy's hand. Mommy's piercing eyes and voice sliced through her heart and froze her in horror. It took only an instant for her to bring back the old, familiar body pose that felt so safe, yet hurt her so. Her chin dropped to her chest and her gaze locked on her toes as the words cut through her body, "Stop your nonsense and settle down! Shame on you for laughing and dancing on the day of his funeral! Don't you care that Billy is dead?"

Her breathing ceased as her world froze for an endless moment. The stabbing pain from such a wound was intercepted by the Spirit, whose wings of compassion gently lifted Billy's picture from Trudy's memory. The pain was tucked in with the other pictures deep inside the imaginary album Billy had given her. The time would come for her to begin walking her path, better prepared to open the buried pages for healing, one at a time.

It has taken fifty more years for the circle to close. The little girl transformed into a woman, wife, mother, and finally grandmother before the awakening. There was no separation by war or pain or time nor even what is called death. It was the glow in her grandson's eyes that lit the path to the reunion of two best friends—Billy and the little girl who continues to live. Their faces appear in windows when the light is just right. At last, they hold hands.

Trudy Patterson, *grandmother, teacher.*

I have always believed that it is not blood which binds us together, but Love . . . and Love never dies.

Dr. Margaret Stortz

DEATH AND SPIRIT

My firsthand experience of death is very limited, indeed. It's a fact of my life, but if it has a meaning, I am unaware of it.

The first death I recall was that of my adored high-school teacher, Lester, who died in New York while I was in Paris on my honeymoon. I was saddened by my sister's letter with the news. Then nothing more . . . until the next day, when "out of the blue" I started to weep, sobbing heavily. Lost, lost without Lester in my universe anymore . . . and I continued to weep for hours until I could accept that I was going to go on with my life. I think the tears stopped finally when I realized that what he had given me during our times together would never die, but would live on in me.

For years, no other deaths.

Then my father, Louis, who was a truly great human being, whose essential goodness I had the good fortune to recognize (with his forbearance and help) some years before his death. When he died, I had a strong awareness that "I was next, wasn't I?"

I prayed that I would make something of a difference to others, even if not as much of a difference as my father had made to the world around him. His meaning in my life goes on. I appreciate him for his compassion, his honesty, and his generosity, which was a matter of life and not policy.

After he built the church for the Afro-American community in his town—out of their need, rather than his self-righteousness—he was called the Saint of Long Beach by some of the parishioners.

I weep every time I recall the story of how the church got built, out of his act of faith in the people rather than any religion. I'm moved to recognize that this immigrant Jewish man had found, and had been in, a state of grace such as I could only wish for myself.

Who was it that said, "after the first death, there are no others"?

Now, through the years, I have been with people in my life who were facing the death of their dear ones, and I have looked in my heart to know what to say. Out of everything that has been given me by teachers, by the writings of the wise, by thoughts from those who inspire, this is what comes to me:

We know from the investigations of science that the energy of which the physical body is made is indestructible. How much more assured we may be then that the Spirit that dwells in us is as indestructible as the substances we are physically made of.

To reinforce this assumption of faith, we have memory— memories of all that the dead have left with us, the living. What they gave to us, left with us, and what remains with us is their Spirit—the Spirit that was in them.

How wholly natural, then, to take comfort in the knowledge that there is no death.

Some months ago I lost consciousness on the street without any warning. I was about to take a step forward in the small, ancient French city where I live . . . then I awoke to find myself lying face-up on the cobblestones with seven or eight concerned faces peering down at me. I had been without consciousness for two minutes, I was told.

As I opened my eyes, they all smiled down on me. They were friends who lived or worked within yards of where I fell. And I felt so blessed to be in the aura of their loving gazes. It was as if I awoke from a dream, was awakened by the call of their love, the love of my neighbors. And it came to me so clearly that there is no death.

When I saw the doctor who tried without success to discover what had befallen me, he asked, "Are you afraid of dying?"

I answered without any hesitation, "No, not at all."

I feel sure that death is a transition, that my Spirit will go on among my friends and loved ones, and that in the end I shall wake up among loving gazes and go on to whatever comes next, supported wholly by love.

Rachmael ben Avram, *teacher, student.*

AN ETERNAL MOMENT

I stood at my Grandma's bed holding her feet. Not caressing or massaging them. Just holding her feet. My left hand on her right foot, right hand on her left foot—extending gratitude for who she was. She appeared to be asleep. There was no indication of awareness or even a willingness to be present in the room as the family gathered to wait and express the love and respect we all felt for her. Her name was Grace, and she had demonstrated that quality as long as I can remember.

Suddenly her head was up, her eyes were wide open and radiant, like the morning sunrise. She held my astonished gaze for a moment and then her voice broke the silence that had darkened and engulfed the room.

"I love you," she said, and an eternity passed between us before she closed her eyes and returned her head to the pillow.

It was only a brief moment, but I will never forget it. In an instant she transformed all of us in the room, moving us from fear and worry about the unknown to a state of grace, dignity, and acceptance of the inevitable. That brief moment has become my companion, one that continues to hold my hand and remind me to stay connected to Spirit.

I am reminded that unexpressed love is our greatest remorse and that the expression of love can transform any situation to a state of dignity and grace—a state that honors and respects our individual and collective vulnerability.

Paul Hinckley, architect and teacher.

"YOU DID A GOOD JOB . . ."

My grandmother was a little roly-poly lady living on the East Coast when she had a stroke. She couldn't move, couldn't talk, and had been hospitalized.

She lost her husband when my mother was two years old and struggled to raise her three children alone through the Depression.

I had flown in from California and was bracing myself, thinking she'd probably lost a lot of weight and wouldn't look very good. I needed to be prepared, so I would not be shocked by her appearance, not let that get in the way of my being there with her.

I remember my mother being very nervous about going to the hospital. She was so uncomfortable about seeing my grandmother that she decided not to go. Since I had a very compelling feeling that I needed to be there and do something for my grandmother, I said, "It's okay, Mom. I'll go. I don't mind. I'll go."

So I went to see my grandmother. I was thinking as I walked from the elevator to her room, "Now what do I need to tell her? What do I need to do or say?"

As I walked into the room, she was lying in the bed and looked fine, certainly not as bad as I had braced myself for. But she couldn't move or talk.

I just took her hand in my hand and sat there with her for a few minutes and I felt her. I felt she was worried. Her face looked worried, and I asked myself once again, "What does she need to know?"

And it came to me. *She needs to know she's done a good job!*

I said to her, "Mom asked me to come. She wanted me to tell you that you did a good job, and I want you to know that Mom did a good job, too. My kids are happy and we really love you. You did a good job. We're very grateful to you."

In that moment she turned her head slightly, squeezed my hand, a tear came down her cheek, and she smiled. She just stayed that way, and I sat with her. We sat in that wonderful feeling.

Shortly after that time we spent together, she died. My mother's brother called with the report from the hospital, and he told my mother, "I will be forever grateful to Patricia. I don't know what she said to Mother, but Mother died with a smile on her face."

Patricia Sun, *philosopher, spiritual teacher.*

REACHING FOR THE ANGELS

"Reaching for the angels" is what the nurses called it when I described my mother's movements. With her outstretched arms and hands, she seemed to be grasping for something out there, reaching toward Heaven.

Carrie Fowler Claycomb Douglas was getting ready to leave her earthly body just before her eighty-eighth birthday.

She quieted and we talked. She had been anxious to see me that morning when I arrived. Her usual greeting, "I'm so glad you're here. I've been waiting for you," was spoken with the deep intensity I had heard each morning and afternoon.

That evening, I stayed until she seemed calm and was ready to go to sleep. It was the same ritual each night. I would kiss her goodbye and say "I love you." She would say, *"And I love you."*

I should have been prepared for the early-morning call saying she was unresponsive, but I wasn't. I hurried to the nursing home, staying by her side all day and holding her hand, not wanting to let go of her hand nor of her. The next morning, she peacefully took her last breath.

I felt that her Spirit was leaving during that day and night, and she knew I was there with her. She welcomed this transition and had spoken of it to me for some time. She was yearning to leave this earthly plane to go be with God and had well prepared herself for the journey.

Today is her birthday and I feel she is with me as I write this. Thanks to dear loving friends, I have been able to let go, not all at one time, but slowly as I have gained a better understanding of what is beyond for me.

Donna Douglas

A WONDROUS WHITE LIGHT

A wondrous white light appeared to me following the death of my beloved daddy. I had been to see my father after receiving a call from my sister informing me that he might not recover from a recent routine operation.

Daddy and I talked a few precious minutes after several days of a silent bedside vigil. In another few days we all felt he would rally. I returned home confident that he was going to be fine. However he didn't rally.

This, my first experience with the death of a close and revered family member, set off abundant anger in me, a rage I had not ever known before. I was angry at myself, at God, even at life itself. It brought up questions from *why are we born?* to *what is life all about?* And more.

Finished with my huge display of angry wailing and pounding the floor and walls, I set myself to the tasks of the funeral, greatly dreading everything about it.

As I lay resting, awaiting the time to leave for the airport, this wonderful white light happened. It was an amazingly bright yet soft light. The light was all-encompassing. It lingered around me. In the midst of the light, I heard my father's voice as clearly as if he were next to me. He said, "I'm all right. Don't worry." As I write this, a delightful little chill comes over me and a sense of great comfort.

This wondrous white light, as I have chosen to call it, and my father's reassuring words completely changed all of my fears and feelings about death. They enabled me to breeze through the funeral with a light heart instead of the sunken, angry, remorseful feelings I had prior to this lovely experience.

Although I think about this wonderful happening often, I have no explanation to offer, for I always *knew* my daddy and I had a very special unspoken way of communicating with each other. Perhaps, however, so do we all. Whatever the explanation, my wish is indeed for everyone to experience this wondrous white light that allowed me to feel assured and completely comfortable and also to feel even light-hearted in the face of the death of my beloved and special daddy.

Jann Walker, *Americorp Vista volunteer, Senior Citizen Programs.*

A blundering despatch, mistakenly announcing the death of a friend, occasions the same grief that the friend's real death would bring. You think that your anguish is occasioned by your loss. Another despatch, correcting this mistake, heals your grief; and you learn that your suffering was merely the result of your belief. Thus it is with all sorrow, sickness and death. You will learn at length that there is no cause for grief, and divine wisdom will then be understood. Error, not truth, produces all the suffering on earth.

Mary Baker Eddy

(This, written by Mrs. Eddy in CHRISTIAN SCIENCE PRACTICE *in the late 1800s, is one of America's early teachings on the transitory nature of death.)*

"PREACHER, CANCEL MY FUNERAL"

I want to relate the story of a remarkable woman whose dying process I had the privilege of assisting. While this woman was visiting from her hometown, her daughter asked me to intervene. I was told that the woman, whom I shall call "Sally," had been raised in mainline Protestant religions. I was not sure how much she knew of my own metaphysical orientation, nor of my spiritual practices.

I found Sally in bed. Though in pain, she was fully oriented and somewhat embarrassed by not being "made-up." She did not seem sure about my visit, and I sensed some resistance. Our initial conversation was superficial. She made reference to her "backsliding." We both smiled much, and our eye contact was brief. Sally revealed that other than imagining heaven or hell, neither of which she was particularly enthused about, she had done little introspection about dying. Before I left, we spent some time in silence, I enunciated a prayer, and she gave me permission to return.

On our second visit, she looked more relaxed, almost eager to talk. I asked about her life. I encouraged the stories of her life. What was it like to grow up in the Midwest? Raising children? Ending her marriage? Growing old? We carefully constructed a bridge between us. As my curiosity peaked, her heart opened. I could begin to sense a softness. I was giving her a clear message: "I am not here to judge you nor inform you. I am here to walk this journey with you."

In subsequent visits, our trust unfolded. There was a safety created which encouraged her. She now revealed her painful memories, her anger and disappointment at the failed periods of her life, her bouts of doubt with God and the Church. She admitted to a void she felt inside, which she feared would not be filled before her death. Reluctantly at first, but with more confidence later, she unraveled her anxieties over her children's future. I could tell we were arriving at the crucial conversation about her death.

In one of our last visits, I arrived one particularly sunny afternoon. She was sitting up, facing the rays pouring through a window. Without much introduction she said, "I am not afraid of dying." However, she was concerned about her children's capacity to accept her departure. We explored her thoughts about what would happen to her after she died. She was delightfully humorous when she said, "Wherever I go, I don't expect I'll change much. They'll just have to put up with me." We strategized different conversations with her children and eventually planned her funeral with her minister back home.

She returned to her hometown, and I lost track of her. Several weeks later, I received a phone call during which she excitedly reported feeling physically better. So much so that when driving by her church, she decided to stop in and cancel the funeral plans she had made with her minister!

We laughed together. She told me about her children and the result of the conversations we had strategized. She reported feeling complete and unsure as to what was left for her to do. I encouraged her to be at peace and enjoy the silence.

That would be the last time I heard directly from Sally. Two weeks later, her daughter informed me that her mother had died, peacefully, surrounded by several of her children.

***Rev. Bernardo Monserrat**, Minister—Church of Religious Science, Santa Fe, New Mexico.*

THE CHILDREN'S PERCEPTIONS

I have had the privilege of being present at the time of "death" on several occasions, beginning in my early childhood. I've observed death from varied perspectives now, and I am deeply grateful. More than once, I have experienced "near-death" events myself.

My respect for differing belief systems has expanded my own beliefs regarding death. I have seen how social conditioning limits our individuality, and the price we pay is too high. From the perspective of the deathbed, it totally loses value. Our last wish is never for more social conditioning.

The honesty of children has been a great resource. Primarily, my work is with children of all ages—children young in years and also those known as "inner children" who live in adult bodies. Most have been abandoned at some point, or not yet discovered.

These are some children's perspectives from my conversations with them regarding death.

After my grandson gave permission to his kindergarten class to call me Grammy, a little girl came to me in private to tell me she couldn't call me Grammy because she already had one in heaven who might feel hurt.

One boy said, "When you die, you can't touch with your finger, or see with your eyes, or talk with your mouth."
"What can you do?" I asked him.
"Everything else," he replied.

"I'm not scared of the dark 'cause when the lights go out, Daddy comes to stay with me till the dark goes away. He couldn't do that when he was alive 'cause Mommy made him sleep with her."

"Mommy told us that Daddy died when he moved to Denver."

"Where do you think he is now?" I asked.

"I already told you. He's in Denver, with his new family."

"When I get lonesome for my Grandpa, I go to our secret place, but I can't tell you where that is 'cause then I won't find it anymore."

". . . anyways, I don't care. Lots of kids don't have a dad. Why should I want one? Mom keeps finding new guys, but none of them stick around. If one ever does, I'm outta here."

"Where will you go?" I asked.

"I don't know. Maybe I'll go find my real dad someplace."

"I think grownups are scared of dying 'cause they forget everything all the time."

"When I miss my sister, I get mad at God."

"I didn't live at home anymore when my brother died. He came to the town where I lived, then to the foot of my bed, to tell me goodbye. Honestly, I saw him, but nobody believes me, because I was young then."

This was my mother's own childhood experience with death.

Trudy Patterson, "Grammy"

THE TRANSITION OF ALOHA

In New Thought circles, including the Unity teachings, the words "transition" or "passing" are uttered far more frequently than "death." I didn't ponder the impact of the distinction until . . .

Having just spent four days in a healing class taught by a visiting ministerial couple, I hastily decided to bid them farewell at the airport. The beautiful Hawaiian tradition of *Aloha* suggests that a loving send-off include a lei.

Due to that last-minute decision, I needed to buy leis at the nearby airport stalls. In the thirty years I've been privileged to live in Hawaii, this was only the second time I'd purchased a lei there, as I prefer making them myself.

As my car approached the dozen rows of colorful lei stands, my intuition guided me to the farthest one. I felt a disturbing energy there and noticed a small crowd. As I walked toward them, my attention shot to a Hawaiian woman in her mid-fifties, lying on the sidewalk. Her long gray hair flailed as she thrashed with what looked to me like an epileptic seizure. A young Filipina lei saleswoman was trying to insert a metal spoon into her mouth, and as she did so the convulsing lady's teeth crumbled on the spoon.

Silently thanking God for the last four days of preparation for this very moment, I felt quite prepared to help. Kneeling beside the Hawaiian woman, praying, I gently embraced her cheeks within my hands. When I touched her, she immediately stilled! She looked so very, very peaceful. I thought, "This healing stuff really works," while continuing to hold her.

I heard the approaching siren of the summoned ambulance. As soon as the paramedics saw the quiet, silent patient, they snapped, "How long has she been this color?"

I said, "I don't know," for this was my first experience with anything like this.

Withdrawing to make room for them, and with bated breath, I watched as they quickly apply the defibrillator shocks to the woman. *No response.* They repeated the current of resuscitation. *No response.* Feverishly sweating in the bright afternoon sun, they injected a needle into her heart. *No response.* Another surging jolt. *No response.* Finally and reluctantly, they declared her dead.

It was my turn to be shocked. She'd seemed so peaceful. I'd thought her seizure had simply ceased.

Recalling my original purpose, I quickly purchased fragrant leis for the departing instructors. Dazed, I proceeded to the terminal. After encircling the ministers with their leis, I recounted the experience I'd just had. Gently, they explained that I'd assisted the woman in making her transition . . . and that this, indeed, was a form of healing.

I still vividly recall her peaceful countenance—her gift to me. It held a knowing of how peaceful death can be and that, truly, rather than an end to life, it is a passing, a crossing over, a transition—into another form of life.

Therese Godfrey, Unity Teacher; Minister, Church of Practical Theology.

SHARED
REFLECTIONS
ON SERVICE

*Ultimately, on this journey, we simply become
compassion, as a natural consequence of what
we have seen and understood.*

Ram Dass

SHARED REFLECTIONS ON SERVICE

THE TRUTH ABOUT GOODBYES

Goodbyes are sad things. We leave behind the dreams we've worked to make real, friends we have suffered with and grown to love, and sometimes a quiet security that was built over what seems to be half a lifetime. In life everywhere, we move along and leave our efforts behind us in the dust, knowing inside that we will never find them exactly the same again. Often we spend too much time looking back and we miss something up ahead. But there is little use in trying to avoid the loneliness and anxiety that go with us when we move on . . . for that is life, and it is a certainty. Life teaches us to accept goodbyes as a part of saying hello to things that are newer. It teaches us also that what was lost was loved . . . and what was learned in the past can never be lost.

Peggy Bassett, D.D., Minister; past President, United Church of Religious Science.

MY FEELINGS ABOUT DEATH

My feelings about death are really quite simple. Like most things, death is basically not complicated anyway and is only made complex by the human tendency to want to comment upon everything. Death is viewed as a kind of oblivion by so many, but in my mind there is no such thing as nonexistence. How can life retreat from any part of itself?

Nothing can be proved to our satisfaction, of course. We can neither prove nor disprove the continuity of life. This is not a matter of science but of faith, as are so many things in the world of spirituality.

In the Western world we keep wanting to make facts out of essences and qualities. I have never felt that death was a fact but rather a transition, which is to say that death is the doorway to change. Someone we loved was once an important part of our lives, and then he or she was gone, the physical sense of that one removed from our experience. Is he removed from our hearts? I hardly think so. Here—and whereinsoever else—he still lives, but the relationship has changed forever.

These are the things we must come to peace with about death. Information may help, and so may some facts, but essentially our greatest healings shall come intuitively . . . known *by* us by becoming known *through* us. And this sense comes through our openness to it, when our wanting to know is greater than our fear of not knowing. We do not have to understand everything. "Why did such a young person die? It isn't right." Who is to say what is right when it comes to the ongoingness called death? It is we who want to decide when one should die. Supposedly when a loved one is sick and "full of years," then we can let him go. But I have seen the elderly grandparent mourned just as deeply as a child cut off in the springtime of life. Perhaps there will always be some difficulty letting loved ones go toward their next steps, and we must not consider such feelings unnatural. Perhaps we must, as Brugh Joy has written, "delete the need to understand" and simply let things be what they are, knowing that after the difficult night of loneliness, the new day always comes.

Maybe then we may say with the philosopher Ernest Holmes, "Our contention is not that dead men live again, *but that a living man never dies.*"

Dr. Margaret Stortz, Minister, Practitioner, Counselor; past Chair of the International Board of Trustees and past President of the United Church of Religious Science.

There will be no more cries when everyone believes that no one truly dies . . .

Gerald Jampolsky & Diane Cirincione

I CAME IN SERVICE

I have had the privilege, honor, and responsibility of being with friends as they began the difficult path of acceptance of their approaching transition from this life. Some I had known for years and some for just a brief few months. I don't think that mattered when it came to building a committed friendship-relationship that allowed total openness and trust to develop as we walked/talked together. I came in service; they could and did take from me just what they needed.

In service, my first obligation is to "empty myself" of all pre-conditionings, all judgments, all rules and regulations, all the daily-grind stuff, and all time-restraints. In the presence of the person, I become totally obligated to them, soul-level to soul-level, with no one and nothing else allowed to interrupt this deep connection. I always center myself by touching my heart and aligning my spirit with Spirit. I enter each visit with as much of my heart-center attributes of compassion, healing presence, innate harmony, and unconditional love as I am capable of bringing forward into this soul connection. I quiet myself and enter.

Sometimes talk is expected, sometimes just a hand, sometimes a shared tear, sometimes a joke or "a dirty story," sometimes a little guided meditation, sometimes a spiritual reading, and sometimes I was needed to clean up a mess. And then we'd laugh; that was always needed! It is all Holy Work for me.

In service, my fears of separation just never seem to pull at my heart. I have moved to another place. I have left my everyday self behind and merged into wholeness. I am seeing a bigger picture, for I have a wider view. It may be only a brief glimpse, but I now know that in service I find my pathway to healing and wholeness . . .

Richard Robinson, RScP, caregiver, student.

BURIED TREASURE

The evening nurse encouraged me to take a break from my bedside vigil. "I'm fine," I answered, much too quickly. But I heard the edginess in my voice as I left you alone.

The hospital cafeteria was nearly empty. I stared at the steam rising from the paper cup and thought about my life before this happened. How many bad cups of coffee has it been, I wondered? How many anxious phone calls? Doctors' appointments? Forms to sign? Trips to the pharmacy? I remembered the litany of complaints that invariably began each caregivers' support group I had attended. *"I feel so alone."* *"My life is on hold."* *"All he ever does is sleep."* Occasionally the unthinkable thought would slip past its barricaded recess deep in the mind and one of us would mutter, *"I wish it were over."* With eyes averted, a circle of heads would respond with barely perceptible nods of agreement.

Tossing back the last of the coffee, I rose and walked to the window overlooking the courtyard. Its curving walkways and reflecting pool contrasted with the efficient bustle of the hospital environment. I remembered something else about the support groups. After our burdens had been shared, we inevitably found ourselves remembering the funny things and then, finally, those incredibly intimate and insightful moments we had all experienced in our caring. As we dug through the rubble of our lives, we discovered the treasures that had been buried.

For example, my sense of time is different. It's as though clocks don't have hands anymore. With life suddenly too precious to measure, it is always "now." This morning as I stepped from my car in the hospital parking lot I paused to enjoy the fragrance of dewy jasmine. Later while I patiently held the cup, time stood still as I watched you gingerly sip the melting ice chips like a fragile hummingbird savoring nectar.

Humor is another treasure I've come to appreciate. Just a few minutes ago, perhaps influenced by the morphine, you said something that made no sense. My attempt to respond was even sillier. We both wound up howling at the absurdity of the situation. It felt so good to laugh at ourselves.

Things that once consumed my attention now seem so trivial. The neighbor's dog still barks, the car window still sticks, and the pharmacy refund check still hasn't arrived, but it all seems so inconsequential in the larger scheme of things. All those goals and affirmations I did for career advancements, salary increases, dream vacations, and things I couldn't live without suddenly seem frivolous. At the same time I am gradually learning to honor myself by being more thoughtful about promises, responsibilities, commitments, and friendships.

Like Dorothy in *The Wizard of Oz*, we caregivers have been sucked up by a twister into a strange land and we yearn to return to our familiar life, but this wicked witch keeps getting in our way. So we're forced to surrender to the adventure and to trust the kindness of strangers. We're doing things we never thought we could do, making decisions we never thought we would have to make, and most of us have never felt so vulnerable. Along with Dorothy's friends Lion, Scarecrow, and Tin Man, we're discovering the depths of our courage, wisdom, and compassion.

It seems caregiving is a *rite of passage*—one that reveals Life's gifts to us as well as the gifts we bring to Life.

Buz Hermes, teacher, counselor, Program Coordinator for Caregivers Support at KAIROS—San Francisco.

DEATH IS AN OLD FRIEND

Death . . . to me is an old friend . . . revisited again and again throughout my long and checkered career. And I smile when I speak these words because death for me has no mystery, has no power, and especially has no abject terror in its finality. When the last curtain call has stilled our life's play, and the last labored gasps have left the tortured remains, it's time to write finis . . . the end . . . oblivion . . . but is it?

I believe, nay, I *know* that life as energy goes on . . . and no one, not even this great, awesome Power we call The Creator, can destroy or terminate the energy of Life. That is the Law of the Absolute. This I know, and the best yet is that each of us has a particle of this indestructible Infinite Power within us, and this power of Life goes on and on.

Certainly the earthly remains return to their unformed components to start new combinations, new steps in the dance of life, but the kernel of indestructible energy within us, the I AM that is expressed in us, as us, up until the experience we recognize as transition, goes on to a new experience . . . new horizons to explore and a new life more wondrous than the last one . . . this I know too.

For those of us who are left behind, for the caregivers, for the selfless multitudes who help the ones that make their transitions, I can give you nothing but my recognition of your valiant efforts, my earnest prayers, and most of all, my love. To do what you do takes a special breed of people whose resolve and selfless help shine brightly in these dark times.

Rev. Victor Postolaki, Minister; Religious Science Fellow and International Outreach Chairman, United Church of Religious Science.

CARE OF THE CAREGIVER

Taking care of the caregiver is more important than one can imagine. In my position as a minister, I have frequently had occasion to bury the caregiver before the one being cared for, and I have often suspected it was in great part because of the simple "wearing out" of the one who cared.

All caregivers must realize that a very infirm person usually cannot consider the needs of those near her. Her world has drawn tightly around her, and she, so to speak, "neither looks to the right nor to the left." Caregivers must come to know that this seeming inconsideration is not intended. The sick person simply cannot help it.

It is important, then, that caregivers regularly consider their own needs for rest and refreshment. As I like to say, "Your name must come to the top of the list, also." To continue one's own good health means that guilt-free "times out" are, in a word, mandatory. It is only wise and loving for caregivers to love themselves enough to meet their own needs so they can return, refreshed, to meet the needs of others.

The finitude in which the caregivers find themselves must be acknowledged and anticipated. While they may know they have a tap into inexhaustible Love, they must remember that their own flesh, bone, and spirit will eventually cry out for relief, and such relief must be taken, not just when the caregivers are at an extreme point, but on a regular basis. To wait for relief to the point of extremity can indicate a bit of hubris. "I am strong. I am deeply spiritual. I am serving God. I can do this." The likely "fall from grace" is just too devastating and discouraging. Better it is, I believe, to think enough of the caring self to give it a break on a regular basis.

There is something special about the person who puts aside a bit of his own life to care for the very ill. No doubt there are hidden blessings and self-awarenesses about the strength and endurance he did not know he had, along with looks of love and gratitude in the eyes of the ones cared for, at least while their situations allow it. All this should lead to the deepest respect for the caregiver—especially for the caregiver's care for himself.

Dr. Margaret Stortz, *Minister, Practitioner, Counselor; past Chair of the International Board of Trustees and past President of the United Church of Religious Science.*

Let each play his part in all he finds to do, with unyoked soul.

The Bhagavad-Gita

WE LET DAD DIE WITH DIGNITY

About six years ago, my mother and I made the most momentous decision of our lives: to let my father die. It was a decision that brought us tremendous grief, but at the same time it led my mother and me to a profound shared experience that was ultimately a great comfort in a time of loss.

In America today, death is considered unacceptable. No matter how serious the illness, how profound the injury, how poor the quality of life will be, we struggle to protect and preserve each life at all cost. And just as strong as our wish that life not end is our desire to separate ourselves from any responsibility for such an event.

Instead, we place matters in the hands of a medical establishment that has little close connection to our personal lives and preferences; we follow guidelines laid down by detached legal entities; or we choose to leave all to fate. In this stepping away, we desert those whom we profess to love the most.

There is no more wrenching decision than to choose death for another. No matter if the dying person has signed a Living Will or how inevitably death looms, making an irreversible decision such as that is indescribably difficult—which is precisely why our responsibility as family members is to take it on.

The U.S. Supreme Court may soon make a ruling on medically-assisted suicide of the terminally ill. But in the arena of life that most of us experience, there will never be a set of unambiguous guidelines. Instead, we independently must find strength to take the action that seems to us most right.

To this day, I regard my father's death as a tragedy and a mystery. But in his loss, my mother and I experienced a gift: the gift of shared love and communion that powerfully united us. My father died quietly, with great dignity, his loved ones at his side. His passing was a traditional family experience—one that too many modern families are denied.

I know my father's life could have been extended to some degree. But the so-called "life" available to him then would have been empty of meaning or satisfaction. And so, with full confidence, my mother and I made the decision to bring it to a close. Accepting so much responsibility was not easy, but for us to take it on was right.

The pain of losing my father is still very much with me. And so is my firm conviction that somewhere he is grateful to us for having let him go.

Michele McCormick, *public relations consultant, writer.*

THE LIGHT OF MOON

It was a sunny afternoon in 1988 when I met Moon. I spotted him in a local animal shelter; his little paw was sticking out through a big, ugly wire fence, straining toward me as far as it could go. He wanted *out*! Not only did he want out, but he also seemed to want me. My response was immediate and instinctive. I posted bail and took him home, holding his little, warm body in my lap.

Moon and I hooked up shortly after a sudden illness had dropped me like a stone. In the prime of my life I was plagued with fatigue, depression, and pain that confined me to my home eighty percent of the time; most of my socializing was in the doctor's office. The illness was chronic and stubborn; my physical movements were intermittent, slow, and deliberate. My life was flat.

As soon as Moon arrived he took over, pretending he didn't know I was sick. His energy was limitless; his curiosity and resourcefulness knew no bounds. No refrigerator was too high a perch, no tall tree too daunting, and certainly a sick woman was no problem at all. He ignored my complaints and simply demanded that I join him in living life fully. Moon loved me unconditionally (unconditionally, except, of course, for having certain food preferences that if not fully met resulted in sulking behavior). Without consciously realizing it, I found that my self-pity faded as Moon and I had fun together; lethargy gave way to increased energy, and my loneliness disappeared as we forged an intimate companionship. Before I knew it, I began to heal and re-enter life.

Fifteen years passed. Moon lived each of those years fully, having fun, sleeping in the sun, climbing and exploring, eating gourmet meals, resting his soft, animal body next to mine. I slowly recovered from my illness.

Then, one day, he returned from his regular mystery walk very sick. I rushed him to the veterinarian, who suggested that he had eaten something toxic. He recovered, but that night I realized his life, like my own, was finite. Philosophically I accepted it. Emotionally I was scared. I couldn't imagine life without Moon; he was my soul-animal, my comfort, and an inexhaustible source of vital life as I had healed. Following that incident he had intervals of illness. Sometimes he would bounce right back, and other times he needed months to recover. Summers were hot, so he decided to live in the tile shower, which cooled his overheated body. Then one day, I realized that not only had he stopped jumping up on the refrigerator, but he was also having difficulty jumping onto the couch. I saw sadness in his face and felt sorrow in my heart.

That day was pivotal, for I accepted that Moon was in the last phase of his life. It was a very difficult step, but I had to tell myself the truth that he was, in fact, dying.

How could I live without Moon, who had helped me to live again? Immediately the answer came. How could I have missed it? The answer was that I had asked the wrong question. The right question was: What can I do *now*, today, while he is still alive, for my beloved friend to whom I owe so much? This answer came easily. What I could do was to help Moon die well.

I took action! Mostly the action was internal. I immediately changed my attitude of fear and uncertainty, which had seeped into our home, contaminating him, covering him prematurely with a shroud. Because he was so attuned to me, I realized the heaviness I saw in his eyes was my own fear reflected back at me. I released Moon from my emotional hovering. I apologized to him and began listening more carefully to what he wanted instead of focusing on my own self-pity. Later there would be time to grieve, but today, *now*, Moon was still alive and needed me for a very specific purpose—as I had needed him so long ago.

Something remarkable happened! As soon as I changed my response to his dying, he immediately lightened up. It was almost as though my shift enabled him to relax into this last phase of his life naturally, without struggle. Each moment for the next two months—even the days when his body was clearly giving up; yes, even the moment his spirit left his body—he was happy, content, and closer to me than he had ever been.

In releasing Moon from my own fear, I believe I freed him to live his dying as well as he had his living. My prayer is that when my own soul's journey is completing itself here and my life is ending, someone will be close by to help me surrender into the natural part of living that is called dying. I hope this friend will be able to meet me fully, to give and receive light and grace from the experience of joining me, unafraid, as I prepare to leave. I trust that someone, whoever it may be, will *receive* the gifts of comfort, love, and renewal that I received, and that I hope I gave to my Moon.

Marsha Mendizza, counselor, coach, teacher.

WHEN ONE DOOR CLOSES . . .

How I view my own death? How could I know the answer to this question until I reach this point in my long life of eighty-seven years? I only *know* that I love Life and I want to continue living, learning, and growing into deeper consciousness. I believe that when one door closes, another opens, and that when I enter the Door of Death, I will step into a new and deeper awareness of who I was and who I may become as I walk in the Light and feel the protective and loving presence of God.

Where my steps will take me, I do not know, but I deeply believe that Life is an ongoing process, and that Death opens the door into a new Life in this ongoing process of Birth-Death-Rebirth, and Living . . .

Shelby Parker, educator, Unity teacher, and teacher of A COURSE IN MIRACLES.

THE EDITOR'S HEARTFELT APPRECIATION

I had the pleasure and privilege of walking a spiritual path with Shelby Parker for many years during the latter part of her life. She had an extraordinary history of enthusiastic openness to self-discovery, and when we talked I felt as though I were in the presence of a master-teacher. She was a one-woman spiritual conference, a living encyclopedia of wisdom. She was also a major mentor in my AIDS fundraising, my guide as I entered into working with palliative care, and my first promoter as I began developing this very book.

Shelby is seeing Life from another view now, for she made her transition not long after writing the words above. She was living and learning and growing into her deeper consciousness right to the moment of gently leaving her beautiful life in Hawaii.

She blessed so many friends and students by being our wise elder and mentor. Many people in the arenas of education, human potential trainings, metaphysical studies, New Thought, and consciousness teachings were nurtured and helped along on their pathways by this very warm and loving teacher. Jean Houston has called her "the Grandmother of the Human Potential Movement."

Among the many notes, letters, and calls I received after her passing was the following from Gerald Jampolsky and Diane Cirincione:

> We would like to share with you a tribute for a very dear friend, a wonderful teacher for us, and a longtime student of *A Course in Miracles.*
>
> Shelby Parker made her transition in September '96 at the age of eighty-eight years young, in Hawaii. Shelby gave us and many, many others another way of looking at life and at the aging process.
>
> Shelby dearly loved the *Course* and with the many challenges in her life, she continued to remind herself that she was not a body, that she was free, and that she was as God created her.
>
> Shelby refused to be limited by form. Rather than thinking that her aging wrinkles were something to be depressed about, she turned the whole thing around and only counted her many and wonderful smile wrinkles.
>
> If there was ever a free spirit, it was Shelby. She had a way of living each moment with flair, with her colorful clothing, her boundless enthusiasm for life that only comes from God.
>
> Shelby traveled all over the world in her quest to expand her own spiritual journey. Along her way she affected thousands of people. She saw herself as more of a student than a teacher and was not fully cognizant of the important role that she played in so many others' lives. She did workshops for children and for adults of all ages. She was very active at Unity Church of Diamond Head, Hawaii, where we saw her play a not insignificant role in

nourishing three different ministers during their tour of duty at the church.

Shelby, your light continues to shine on all of us. We thank you for your light, wisdom, and humor, and for your willingness to be ever present.

I was privileged to have been a member of Shelby's "Mainland family," a group of people with whom she gathered during her trips to California's Bay Area. Among those I telephoned with the news of her passing were two other members of this "family," who sent the following notes:

Dear Richard,
    I appreciate your call letting us know about Shelby. No matter what her mind has to say, her soul is ready . . .
    A radiance of Love,
    Brugh Joy

Dear Richard,
    Both of us have been blessed to know Shelby, and now she has moved on . . .
    Ram Dass

Shelby had to have her left foot amputated in July 1996, and we had many long phone calls about her life following this loss. She had a difficult time not being "free to go, do, and walk." After we'd spent some time in prayer together one evening, sitting on her lanai in the full rapture of a Hawaiian sunset, she told me, as tears flowed in her eyes and mine, that she had always wanted to be a dancer . . .

After Shelby's transition, Eric, her son and God-sent caregiver, phoned Elisabeth Kubler-Ross, one of Shelby's dearest friends, to inform her. Two days later Elisabeth called Eric back saying she knew Shelby was in a wonderful place, having a great time—and dancing . . .

Richard Robinson, *friend of Shelby Parker.*

THE END OF THE PLAY

I have often thought of my own death as:

THE END OF THE PLAY

The final curtain descends.
The applause is over.
I go to my dressing room and remove my makeup.
The costume is left on the floor.
The character is no longer me.
Naked I walk to the stage door.
As I open the door I am met by a smiling face.
It is the new Director,
new script and costume in hand.
I am overjoyed to see all my loyal fans and loved ones
waiting.
The applause is loving and deafening.
I am greeted with more love than I have ever experienced
before.
My new role promises to be the most exciting ever.

I know
Life is always good
Wherever I am
All is well
I am safe
see you later
'Bye

Louise L. Hay, *author, teacher, lecturer, and publisher.*

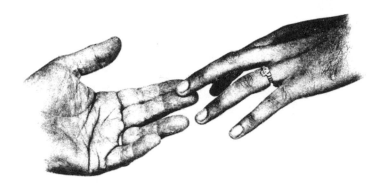

Death loses its sting, the grave its victory, when we realize the eternity of our own being. Nature will not let us stay in any one place too long. She allows us to stay just long enough to gather the experience necessary to the unfolding and advancement of the soul. This is wise, for should we stay here too long, we would become too set, too rigid, too inflexible. She demands the change in order that we may advance. When the change comes we should welcome it with a smile on the lips and a song in the heart.

Dr. Ernest Holmes, author of *The Science of Mind*

RANDOM THOUGHTS

Here are random thoughts I bring forward just as if we were sitting together in a circle, a kiev, gathered around sharing stories—for in a certain way we are.

I've had many middle-of-the-night feelings and insights about this book and the whole project that surrounds its purpose. Once when I was at a conference with Brugh Joy, he talked about how the first sensation a newborn experiences at birth, after light, is *touching and being touched.* I remember flashing on the thought that if touch was our first body-experience with connection to the world, even before nourishment from our mother's breast, then *why shouldn't touch be our final experience*, as we make our transition? I liked the alpha and omega, the beginning and ending this connection held for me. Therefore, *holding another's hand* as they prepare to leave this plane of life seemed to become my personal message and my pledge.

So many teachers, human and nonhuman, have added to the tapestry of my studies of life, death, and palliative care as I put my full intention to this project. They include:

Stewart Emery, who told me in a graduation group that the biggest workshop I would ever experience was called *Life*.

Wayne Dyer, who came along to teach me about *being on purpose* in my life when I started thinking and talking about this book and the whole project it encompasses.

The book, in fact, seems to have been driving me to get itself created.

My intention has always been that it stay centered in the spiritual and the transcendental, in the compassion given in hospice, nursing homes, or, ideally, one's own bedroom through palliative care, that one-on-one time preceding and during the transitioning process. Yet there are several matters—more objective than subjective, more procedural than palliative—that can be handled with greater ease when the appropriate documents have been put in place by or for an individual. They include a *Durable Power of Attorney— Health & Care*, a *Living Will*, and the newest one, a genuinely heartfelt personal tool, an *Ethical Will*.

I will describe these three documents only briefly here, offering quick suggestions as to how they might help bring reassurance and peace to any transition in process. You will find a wealth of detailed legal information in the many other books and forms available in the "Death and Dying" sections of libraries and bookstores, and on the Internet.

Durable Power of Attorney—Health & Care. Gives another person the legal right to act on your behalf in making your health-care decisions if or when you are unable to do so yourself.

Advance Directive for Health Care. Often called a *Living Will,* this provides further instructions on your desire regarding being kept (or not kept) on life-support or to receive (or not receive) tube feedings.

Ethical Will. Offers a chance for writing about or making a voice recording (or video recording) of the details of one's life story and legacy. It can bring forward whatever needs to be shared with family members and close friends. Here the untold or unfinished stories get revealed/released, as do accounts of family lineage, clan history, religious creeds, immigrant adventures, generational shifts, marriages, others' deaths, important dates, family traditions, and family principles and mores . . . all those things that used to be handed down by grandparents to parents and then to the children— when we lived in closer community to one another.

In the creation of an Ethical Will, you—as the caregiver—may be asked to be "the gatekeeper," who gets the assignment of directing the positive stories and helpful tales that will be passed forward and who may also feel a call to "filter" or "soften" any revelations that might be hurtful or vengeful toward other individuals, living or dead. This wonderful new tool for assisting the release and a peace-full transition is now available from insightful caregivers/authors in numerous books and other publications.

I have personally been *holding hands* now for many years. Initially, I was fear-full, feeling inadequately trained and uneducated, as I had neither formal psychological training nor letters after my name. At times, I remember thinking I was in over my head and I often was awash in emotions/feelings. But I always tried to remember these two important dictums: *First, do no harm* (thought to have originated within the Greek physician's oath), and *The Consolamentum*, the prayer of release. This prayer, offered by the caregiver, is for all anguish and sorrow to be released and for solace and comfort to be present. It asks that the caregiver be peace-full and at-one with whatever is meant to be or to occur in the present situation, becoming the witness to the moment at hand and seeing it manifest naturally, surrendering to The Divine Mystery.

When I am with those who are leaving, or who are soon to leave, I quiet and center myself and then gently move forward . . . or I just sit and hold their hand. I have learned to do and deal with things I previously thought I couldn't do or deal with. Oftentimes, as you do this work, you bite your tongue, stifle a tear, hold your breath, even gag. *But whatever you see that needs your attention, you are there and you give of yourself as best you can . . .*

I hope these pages bring new insight, comfort, reassurance, and serenity to everyone—to all caregivers, all professional attendants, and all those whose hands we hold . . .

Richard Robinson, RScP, *caregiver.*

QUANTUM ET SOLACE

It may just be that when all is

said and done, that the only thing

we can give one another is a genuine

interest and caring for each other's

well-being. Making a commitment

to each other's well-being is not to seek

an escape from living and life. We

seek support, companionship, passion

and compassion for the adventure . . .

love and a sense of humor regarding

the lessons each have to learn . . . and

for the revelation of our own foolishness.

This is an enormous commitment.

Stewart Emery, *teacher, author*

There is this story handed down by caregivers, one to another, about being "simply human" in contact with another as they phase out of this lifetime. Trying to read inspirational material to his frail and not so patient client the caregiver is told, "No please! No more readings. I only want what is in your own mind and heart."

Unknown

A Call to Service

Holding Another's Hand is more than this book title. It is a work in progress that I hope engages many to serve those they see in need during their transition time. Death comes to each of us that are born into this thing called Life. We need each other to be there, to help ease the way, to make it all less fearful. Each of us, no matter what our backgrounds, all have the ability to sit with, to be with, and to bring empathy, compassion, and "a gentle heart" into the dying process and time. We do this with the full awareness of being in the moment, fully attuned to this Sacred time of transitioning from one Life experience to the next Life experience, and we do it all with an open heart. We are aware that we too will one day be in this same transition experience.

If this Sacred Service is important to you or to a group you are part of, you might consider the teachings, recollections, and reflections within these pages to be your facilitator in efforts to train others in Pastoral Care or Palliative Care. This book and the workshops that have been created around these shared stories can also help to generate funds for your particular service work or group.

If you are interested in more information for yourself or for your organization, you may fax, write, or e-mail Richard Robinson in care of Juniper Springs Press.

Juniper Springs Press
P.O. Box 1385
Apple Valley, CA 92356
Fax: (760) 247-5884
E-mail: Publish@JuniperSpringsPress.com

The Hands Photographs

Throughout the pages of this book, I have included pho-
tographs of hands holding hands. They will, I hope, provide a
simple, graphic symbol of just how easily we can demon-
strate care, empathy, and compassion for one another. These
symbolic hands also give you, the reader, visual relief and a
resting place from all the words of wisdom.

And the Photographer

The hands were photographed by Timothy Buchanan. A longtime friend of mine, he is an artist, musician, Christian metaphysician, and dedicated student of Life. He uses his didgeridoo, an Australian Aboriginal musical instrument, for his meditations to center himself and connect his Soul to Spirit. Timothy is involved in service to his community, working with other men working on adolescent drug problems. He serves in many ways through his talents and his gifts, *and* he remembers growing pumpkins around age five and "giving them to everybody in our neighborhood."

I am grateful to Timothy and to all these hands of friends who stepped forward to help in this book project . . .

Richard Robinson

Wisdom Quotations & Hands Photos

RESOURCES

Various resources are available from many of the writers and teachers who contributed to this book. You are invited to contact them directly for more information about their work and/or their teachings.

Angeles Arrien—books, tapes, workshops
P.O. Box 2077, Sausalito, CA 94966
(415) 331-5050, fax (415) 331-5069, www.angelesarrien.com

Maria Elena Cairo—Mexico-Mayan Shamanic Trainings and Healing Journeys; tapes, weekend and residential retreats, phone consultations
4702 N 36th St., Phoenix, AZ 85018
(602) 957-3740, www.mariaelenacairo.com

Ram Dass—books and tapes by Ram Dass and tapes from the Hanuman Foundation Tape Library
524 San Anselmo Ave., San Anselmo, CA 94960
(800) 248-1008, fax (415) 454-4143

Louise L. Hay / Hay House Publications, Inc.—books, audiotapes, videotapes
P.O. Box 5100, Carlsbad, CA 92018-5100
(800) 654-5126, fax (800) 650-5115, www.hayhouse.com

W. Brugh Joy, M.D.—books, tapes, CDs, weekend and residential conferences
P.O. Box H, Marysville, CA 95901
(800) 448-9187, fax (720) 488-9748, www.brughjoy.com

Marsha Mendizza—audiotapes, workshops
13351-D Riverside Drive #194
Sherman Oaks, CA 91423
www.Marsha-Mendizza.com
e-mail: info@Marsha-Mendizza.com

Rev. Bernardo Monserrat—tapes
Church of Religious Science, Santa Fe
505 Camino de los Marquez, Santa Fe, NM 87501
(505) 983-5022

Dr. Margaret Stortz—books, audiotapes, private consultations
741 Colusa Ave., El Cerrito, CA 94530
(510) 524-7901, e-mail: QweenMeg@aol.com

Patricia Sun—tapes, private consultations
P.O. Box 7065 Berkeley, CA 94707
(510) 843-7100

Eliot Jay Rosen—book, videotape
c/o Hay House, P.O. Box 5100, Carlsbad, CA 92018-5100
(800) 654-5126, fax (800) 650-5115, www.hayhouse.com

Richard Robinson, RScP—author, *Holding Another's Hand*;
fundraising information, workshops, private consultations
1200 Lakeshore Ave., Oakland, CA 94606

It is not the great things you do that matter, but the small things you do with great heart.

Mother Teresa

FLOW

Be
as water is,
without friction.

Flow around the edges
of those within your path.
Surround within your ever-moving depths
those who come to rest there—
enfold them,
while never for a moment holding on.

Accept whatever distance
others are moved within your flow.
Be with them gently
as far as they allow your strength to take them,
and fill with your own being
the remaining space when they are left behind.

When dropping down life's rapids,
froth and bubble into fragments if you must,
knowing that the one of you now many
will just as many times be one again.

And when you've gone as far as you can go,
quietly await your next beginning.

Noel McInnis, *Minister, Church of Religious Science, the author of "Flow," has graciously given permission for readers to cut out and photocopy this page if they wish and to share it freely with others.*

INDEX OF CONTRIBUTORS

A dying man needs to die as a sleepy man needs to sleep, and there comes a time when it is wrong, as well as useless, to resist.

Stewart Alsop

About the Editor

Richard Robinson—who conceived, compiled, and edited *Holding Another's Hand*—was born in the heartland of Nebraska and raised in California.

He first ventured into the mysteries of Spirit and Life in 1954 while a student at Art Center School in Los Angeles. His initial studies in Eschatology were followed by Religious Science, and then, as he describes it, "the journey was on—into many other teachings and trainings in the Human Potential Movement, and in workings of the Heart and Soul."

As an executive in retail advertising and sales promotion, he was early to see the devastation AIDS was causing to his creative teams and to all of the fashion industries. Starting with a small group of friends, he formed AMITZVAH, a transformational teaching-lecture and fundraising organization dedicated to producing healing workshops and teachings that generated funds for care and support groups for AIDS clients. AMITZVAH has produced these events with teachers such as Louise Hay, Jerry Florence, and Brugh Joy.

In addition to his ongoing work as a Religious Science Practitioner, Richard is a speaker and a designer/presenter of workshops that focus on healing the fears surrounding the time when life moves on to another expression. This book is an extension of that work. It is a compilation of important teachings—bringing together many voices in a friendly format with easy-to-grasp language—for all caregivers and those who may take on this Sacred Work of holding another's hand as they face the transition called death.

Richard lives in Oakland, California.

My Notes